The Ultimate Guide to
Wilderness Navigation

The Ultimate Guide
to Wilderness Navigation

Cliff Jacobson, Scottie Barnes, James Churchill

THE LYONS PRESS
GUILFORD, CONNECTICUT
AN IMPRINT OF THE GLOBE PEQUOT PRESS

10 9 8 7 6 5 4 3 2 1

Printed in the United States of America

Library of Congress Cataloging-in-Publication Data is available on file.

ISBN 1-58574-490-5

Part I photos courtesy of Suunto, Silva, and the Brunton Company.
Part II photos courtesy Scottie Barnes, Lowrance Electronics, Garmin, Magellan, and the Yeoman Group.
Part III photographs courtesy James Churchill.

Contents

Appendices

Glossaries

Acknowledgments

The Lyons Press is grateful to the authors for their efforts and enthusiasm in researching and writing their respective titles. We hope that in unifying these three popular works we've created a single eminently useful volume.

I'm indebted to Bjorn Kjellstrom, inventor of the Silva Compass, for the historical information in chapter 3.

—Cliff Jacobson

Just as a GPS receiver cannot operate on its own without a little help from its friends in orbit, so too must an author rely upon the gracious assistance of others. I would like to acknowledge Glenn Gibbons, Guy Maynard, and Pete Peterson, without whom I could never have written this book. Thank you all.

—Scottie Barnes

Introduction

On a late-November deer hunt in the Allagash region of Maine a few years ago, five of us paddled canoes deep into the wilderness and set up camp near the West Branch of the Penobscot. The temperatures plummeted on our first night there, going from the 40s to below 0°F.

The first day hunting, we all went our separate ways, following old logging roads, still-hunting the edges of clearcuts, watching open areas deep in the woods. By 3:00 P.M., I had wandered probably 4 miles from camp. I was using a map and keeping a close eye on my compass. But at one point, seeing a big buck moving down a trail maybe 500 yards away, I broke off my planned route and tried to circle way around through a thick conifer forest to get a shot. By the time I reached my intended ambush spot, the buck was gone, and it was close to 4:00. I was unsure of my position—everywhere I looked, all I could see were dark, thickly packed fir trees. A bitter wind knifed at my face as I looked at my compass, which told me I was heading south. Impossible, I thought, I'm facing east. That reading couldn't be correct! I promptly headed off in the direction I was certain was east. The sun was obscured by a darkening gray sky; and the temperature, according to the thermometer hanging off my pack, was 5°F.

Survival experts will tell you not to panic when you become disoriented. When I realized that I was truly turned around, deep in the woods with no one within miles, I panicked, and started stumbling blindly through the woods, searching desperately for a way out. My mind raced—I was lost, it was bitterly cold, I was going to die! Finally, I got a grip on myself. I did not know where my backtrail was, so I decided to just sit down on the frozen ground for a few minutes and think. Slowly I calmed down. In my pack, I had an extra pair of gloves, some granola, jerky, and water, plus a flashlight and matches. I knew that if I had to stay in the woods overnight, I had a good chance of making it. But I also figured that if I could just make my way back to the river, I could find our camp. I heard a tributary nearby, and followed it downhill through incredibly thick stuff, in the dark, in the cold, at one point crunching my way through a frozen bog. But I eventually made it to the river, and then, after looking at my compass and trusting it, I started to hike east, according to my compass, in a downstream direction. Eventually, I made it back to camp—to burning Coleman lanterns, a warm fire, and my companions. They had been worried, they said, but knew that they couldn't begin to look for me until morning.

Three days later, three days of fruitless hunting, the river was beginning to freeze solid. Getting back to camp around 5:00 P.M., we held a brief meeting and decided we had better break camp that evening, or risk having to hike out and leave the canoes until spring. After a quick dinner, we packed the gear and started paddling. Rounding the first bend in the river, under a full moon and with the air impossibly cold, the lead canoe suddenly came to a halt. Ice was blocking the river.

And so began a long ordeal of ice-breaking our way out of the wilderness. Taking turns, the two guys in the lead canoe would paddle hard and crash into the half-inch-thick ice, jamming the bow up on top of it. The man in the bow would then jump up and down, crashing the canoe down through the ice. It was a long, hard evening, but with numb fingers and faces, we finally got back to our trucks—exhausted.

The following year the five of us went back, and I actually got a buck. But getting a deer wasn't the only reason we wanted to return. We also went for the camaraderie. And just as important, we went to test ourselves against the elements, to venture out in the woods on our own each day, knowing that if we messed up, we could pay with our lives. A hunt—or any kind of trip—into the deep woods, where getting lost is easy if you let your concentration stray for one minute, is the type of extreme trip you make just because it's good to be alive, and good to remind yourself of that.

That trip was made when GPS (global positioning system) units were first becoming popular. We didn't have any, because we didn't know what they could do. We had compasses and maps, and we knew how to use them. In my case, I didn't trust my compass—breaking the first rule of using a compass. It's never wrong—trust it, and it will take you where you want to go.

So will a GPS unit. With GPS, you can not only find your way through the woods and waters, you can direct yourself with pinpoint precision to anywhere in the backcountry—to a good hunting or fishing spot that you found last year and entered the coordinates into your GPS; to a backcountry lake that you've never been to, but have the coordinates for; to pristine hiking trails that few others know about.

In this book you'll learn not only how to use your map and compass, but also how to use your GPS in conjunction with them. Using both tools efficiently, you'll never get lost again. But even if you for some reason do, or if you find yourself in a spot where it's best to stay put until daylight, the last section of this book will tell you how to survive the night, or a number of nights—how to make shelter, stay warm, and find food and drink.

A compilation of three Basic Essentials books, on GPS, map and compass, and survival, this book is for anyone who ventures into the backcountry—for a week, a day, an afternoon. Keep it in your pack—you will use it.

—Jay Cassell

Jay Cassell, author, *North America's Big Game Lodges and Outfitters (with John Rossi)*; *North America's Greatest Whitetail Lodges & Outfitters (with Peter Fiduccia)*; and editor, *The Quotable Hunter (with Peter Fiduccia)*; *The Best of Sports Afield: The Greatest Outdoor Writing of the 20th Century*

Part I

Map & Compass

Maps
Getting Started

What You'll Need

It's pointless to begin the study of wilderness route-finding without the two most important tools—a map and compass. So before you begin your study, please assemble the following materials.

1. An orienteering-style compass. No other type works as well. Indeed, you will be *severely* handicapped by any other instrument! You'll find a thorough discussion of compasses in chapter 3. Excellent orienteering compasses are available from these companies:

   Silva Division
   Johnson Camping, Inc.
   P.O. Box 966
   Binghamton, NY 13902
   (607) 779-2200

   Suunto U.S.A.
   Optimus, Inc.
   2151 Las Palmas Drive
   Carlsbad, CA 92009
   (619) 931-6788

   Brunton/Lakota, Inc.
   620 East Monroe Avenue
   Riverton, WY 82501
   (307) 856-6559

2. Space and cost considerations prevent us from including a colored topographic practice map. Instead, we've downsized selected portions of full-size maps, pinpointing the information you need to know. While this should pose no learning difficulty, you may get the big

picture more quickly if you have on hand a genuine topographic map that contains all the pieces of the puzzle on a single page. Any topo map will do, though, and the larger the scale, the better. A 1:24,000 (about 2.5 inches to the mile) American map, or a 1:50,000 (1.25 inches equals one mile) Canadian map is ideal. Why not get a map of your favorite hunting, fishing, or hiking area? Chapter 1 tells you how to order maps.

3. An inexpensive plastic protractor is a must if you don't have an orienteering-style compass. Otherwise, it's surplus baggage.

An Essential Tool

A good map is *everything*. A compass alone won't do. A compass is useful *only if* you know where it leads you. And for that you need a map.

Even a simple state park or road map is better than no map at all. Example: Assume you're lost in a heavily-wooded area. You have a compass but no map and no idea where you parked your car or "went in." Being lost comes as quite a surprise. After all, you hadn't planned on going in "that far."

Realistic problems? You bet! Ask any excited deer hunter. Think hard. How can you find your way out of the woods?

There is one way. It's called *luck*. Maybe if you go in a straight line (on any compass bearing) far enough, you'll hit a road. Maybe!

Now let's redo the problem with the aid of a highway map (figure 1-1). Only this time we can be more specific. You're cruising south on Highway 24 toward Leadville. You park somewhere along the roadway then strike off roughly northeast into the bush. You stuff map and compass deep into your pockets. Surely you won't need them. After all, you're going only "a short distance."

Several hours later, your enthusiasm dampens. Edged against a stand of impenetrable pines, miles of "nothing" stand between you and your car. Now what?

Your highway map shows that roads border the woods all around. Granted, there's not much detail, but it's enough. A rough southwest bearing will bring you back to Highway 24. From then on, it's simply a matter of asking directions.

As you can see, even a gas station highway map or state park guide will get you "out of the woods," if you have a compass and can use it for finding rough directions.

A Matter of Scale

Some years ago, while on a canoe trip in the Boundary Waters Canoe Area of Minnesota, I rounded a point and saw a young couple sitting dolefully on a rock, staring intently at what appeared to be a map. When they saw me, the pair stood up and waved frantically in my direction. Curiously, I paddled over, only to discover the two were hopelessly lost.

The man told me they'd left the lodge the day before and had set out with a complement of backpacking gear to hike a portion of the Kekakabic Trail—an old fire road that runs from Ely to Grand Marais. The trail crosses a number of area lakes, hence our chance meeting. But the trail is poorly marked, and it's not maintained. Numerous animal trails and canoe portages intersect the route and confuse things considerably. A good compass and topo map are essential tools for navigating the "Kek."

The man poured coffee while the woman continued to study the map. "I think we're here," she said, tapping her finger on what appeared to be a small knoll near the water's edge. Eagerly, she looked to me for reinforcement.

I squinted wonderingly at the impossibly small scale (1:500,000) map. Even with my bifocals, I could tell nothing.

"Where'd you get this map?" I questioned.

"From our outfitter," came the reply.

"Hmmm . . ." I walked back to the canoe and got my 1:50,000 topo map and spread it out on the lichen-splashed outcrop.

"I believe you're here," I said, pointing to a drumlin some distance from the perceived location. "How can you guys find your way around up here with a map like this?"

"We can't!" came the ready answer. "Our outfitter said this was all we needed, that it'd work fine."

"Yeah," I replied.

Fortunately, I had three sets of maps in my party, so parting with one caused no inconvenience.

As the case illustrates, you can't do good work without the right tools.

— Cliff Jacobson

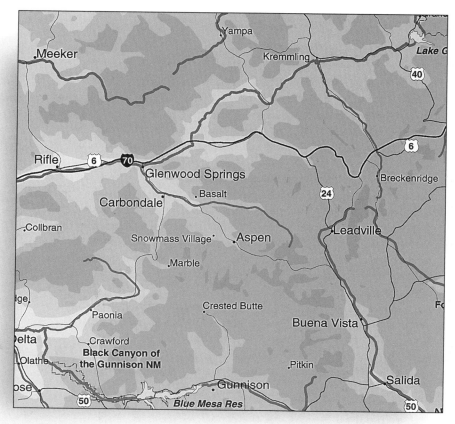

Figure 1-1

Road map of the Aspen area.

Beyond Planimetric Maps

The trouble with road maps (figure 1-1) and state park guides is that they're *planimetric,* which means they show topography in a dead-flat perspective. Hills and valleys don't mean much when you're driving a car. But put on your hiking boots and the mood changes. For cross-country—indeed *any*—wilderness travel, you need a map that shows all the ups and downs plus major stoppers such as swamps and canyon walls. *Topographic* maps, as they are called, provide a three-dimensional perspective of the land.

Topographic Map Scales

All modern maps are made from aerial photographs that give a precise picture of the land. Cartographers (mapmakers) use these photos to construct topographic maps in a variety of scales, the most common of which are summarized below. (Hint: Large scale means "large" detail; small scale, "small" detail.)

For American Maps

1:250,000 (1/250,000): One unit on the map equals 250,000 units on the ground. Each map covers one degree of latitude and two degrees of longitude (see discussion of latitude and longitude in the next section.) We Americans still work and think in the English system and our maps reflect our bias toward inches and feet. Here, 1 inch on the map equals 250,000 inches, or almost exactly 4 miles on the ground. As you might guess, one to a quarter-million maps don't show much detail.

1:62,500: Also called "15 minutes series," each map covers 15 minutes of latitude and 15 minutes of longitude. There are 63,360 inches to the mile, close enough so that 1 inch approximately equals 1 mile. This is probably the most useful and practical scale for backcountry use.

1:24,000 (7.5 minute series): 1 inch on the map equals 2,000 feet on the ground. Works out to a bit more than 2½ inches to the mile. These large-scale maps are great for precision navigation, but each one covers only about 55 square miles of territory, which means you'll need a lot of them if you're traveling very far. And at around three bucks per sheet, costs mount quickly.

For Canadian Maps

1:250,000 (same as American maps) and *1:50,000* are the most popular *traveling* maps in Canada. The 1:50s are particularly nice: Here, 1¼ inches equal one mile.

Colored or Monochrome?

Canadian maps in 1:50,000 scale are often available in monochrome (black and white) as well as colored editions. Consequently, forests (commonly shown as green areas) and lakes (colored blue) will appear in varying shades of gray.

Why get monochrome maps if colored ones are available? Two reasons: they cost less and photocopy better—important considerations if you need a lot of maps or duplications of certain sheets.

Unfortunately, American maps are not available in monochrome editions.

Land Use Information Series Maps

These are standard 1:250,000 Canadian topo maps that are over-printed with information about wildlife, vegetation, hunting and fishing, climate, and points of interest. They'll tell you where peregrine falcons nest, the migration routes and movements of caribou, the location of various fish species, and more. Land use maps tend to be pretty cluttered with data, so they're only marginally useful for navigation.

These maps are not available for all of Canada. Ask for the special Index to Land Use Information Series maps when you write the Canada Map Office.

Land Use and Land Cover Maps

These American maps are similar to Canadian Land Use Information maps, with these exceptions: *Land use* refers to how man's activities affect the land (for example, housing and industry). *Land cover* describes the vegetation, water, and artificial constructions on the land surface. Scale is 1:100,000 or 1:250,000.

Where to Order Maps

A great place to start your search for maps is the website of the U.S. Geological Survey, which provides a host of options. Go to http://mapping.usgs.gov/, or order American topographic maps from:

Branch of Distribution
U.S. Geological Survey
Box 25286, Federal Center
Denver, CO 80225

You can also get quick access to topographic maps at www.topozone.com, which has worked with the USGS to create an interactive topo map of the entire United States. You can find more on this in chapter 10.

For charts and tide tables of U.S. coasts, the Great Lakes, sections of major rivers, and contoured fishing maps write:

National Oceanic and Atmospheric Administration/National Ocean Survey
(NOAA/NOS)
Map & Chart Information, Distribution Branch N/CG33
Riverdale, MD 20737
(301) 436-6990

The Earth Science Information Center (ESIC) will help you find special-purpose maps and aerial photos (including space photos) of all kinds. It sorts and collects cartographic information from federal, state, and local government agencies. Write or call the ESIC office nearest you for a listing of city, county, and U.S. national park maps. National forest maps must be obtained from the U.S. Forest Service district office that manages the national forest of your interest. Your post office or public library can provide addresses. The ESIC will answer all your map questions and tell you what you need. They have a ton (well, at least five pounds!) of free pamphlets. You may phone for information, but you must order maps by mail.

ESIC Headquarters
Earth Science Information Center
U.S. Geological Survey
507 National Center
Reston, VA 22092
1-800-USA MAPS

Western Mapping Center, ESIC
U.S. Geological Survey
345 Middlefield Road
Melo Park, CA 94025
(415) 329-4309

Rocky Mountain Mapping Center, ESIC
U.S. Geological Survey, Box 25046
Denver, Federal Center, Mail Stop 504
Denver, CO 80225
(303) 236-5829

Midcontinental Mapping Center, ESIC
U.S. Geological Survey
1400 Independence Road
Rolla, MO 65401
(314) 341-0851

On the web, the Centre of Topographic Information provides a wonderful starting point for finding the Canadian topos you need: http://maps.nrcan.gc.ca/. You can also buy Canadian topographic maps through a U.S. or Canadian map distributor. Write or call the Canada Map Office for a list of distributors. Canoeists should request the free pamphlet "Maps and Wilderness Canoeing."

Canada Map Office
Department of Energy, Mines, and Resources
615 Booth Street
Ottawa, Ontario Canada K1A 0E9
1-800-465-6277

For Canadian charts and tide tables:

Hydrographic Chart Distribution Office
Department of Fisheries and Oceans
1675 Russell Road, P.O. Box 8080
Ottawa, Ontario Canada K1G 3H6
(613) 988-4931, 32, 33
Fax (613) 998-1217

You can't order maps until you know what's in print. For this, you'll need an *Index to Topographic Maps,* available *free* from the agencies above. Write or call the USGS office in Denver or any ESIC office for American topographic map indexes. The Canada Map Office in Ottawa is your source for indexes to Canadian topographic maps and aerial photos. To get the right index, simply specify the state, province, or geographical region of interest.

When your index arrives, you're ready to order maps. Follow the detailed ordering instructions that come with each index, and you'll have no trouble finding the map you need in the scale you want.

Using Your Map

With your topo map in hand, you're ready to plan your route into the backcountry. Let's begin by identifying the important map features.

Map name: You'll find the map name in the upper and lower margins of American maps, and in the lower margin of Canadian maps. American maps also have names in parentheses that indicate adjacent quadrangles. For example, the map just southeast of ASPEN, COLO. (figure 1-2) is NEW YORK PEAK.

The Canadians use a slightly different system (figure 1-3). Here, the NAKINA name and location designation (42L) are included in a block diagram in the legend—a procedure that allows you to see the adjacent map sheets at a glance.

Scale: You'll find the representative fraction (1:24,000, etc.) and bar scale in the lower map margin.

Date: Most topo maps are very old; some were last field-checked in the 1950s. A lot has changed since then, especially the location of roads, dams, and other man-made features. The key words *revised* and *field-checked* will tell you when these maps were last updated. Certainly, an old topo map is better than none at all. But it won't do if you're planning a remote hunting or fishing trip. If you need more current information than that supplied by your map, contact the government agency (U.S. Forest Service, Department of Natural Resources, etc.) nearest your area of concern. These professionals require current maps for their daily work. If they can't tell you where to get the maps you need, they'll help you update yours.

Latitude and Longitude: Your map is a bird's-eye view of a tiny portion of the earth's surface. But where does it fit onto the "big sphere"? By using *latitude* and *longitude* we can reference any location to a precise spot on the globe.

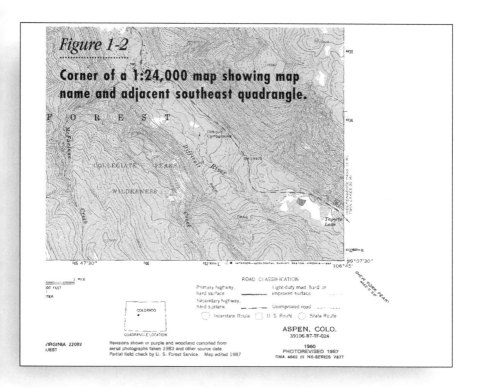

Figure 1-2

Corner of a 1:24,000 map showing map name and adjacent southeast quadrangle.

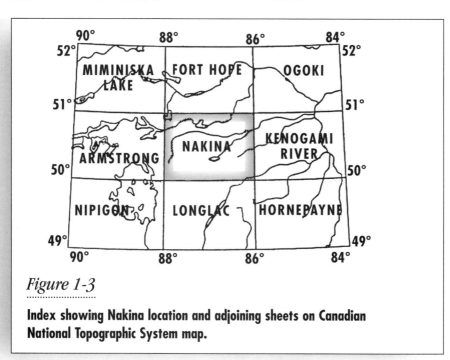

Figure 1-3

Index showing Nakina location and adjoining sheets on Canadian National Topographic System map.

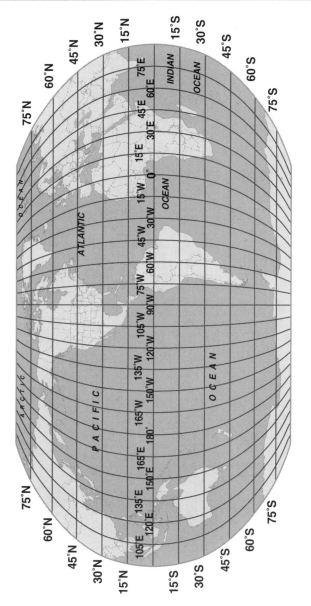

Figure 1-4

Lines of latitude run parallel to the equator. Lines of longitude run north–south and intersect at the poles.

Lines of latitude (or parallels) run parallel to the equator, which is zero degrees. The *longitudinal* (north/south) lines that intersect at the poles are called *meridians,* or lines of longitude (figure 1-4). Longitude is measured in degrees east or west of the zero degree *prime meridian,* which originates in Greenwich, England.

By splitting latitude and longitude degree readings into smaller units, called *minutes* and *seconds,* specific points on the earth may be accurately located via a coordinate system. The rules are simple:

1° (degree) = 60' (minutes)
1' (minute) = 60" (seconds)

For example, Denver (see figure 1-5) is located at approximately 105° west longitude/39° 45' north latitude.

All this is needlessly academic, unless you plan to order specific large-scale maps and *aerial photographs.*

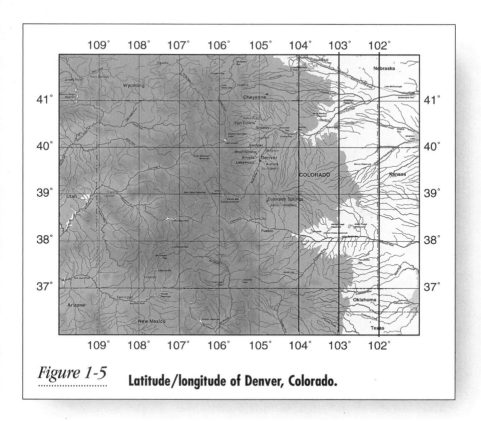

Figure 1-5   **Latitude/longitude of Denver, Colorado.**

Aerial Photos

Suppose you're planning to canoe a remote river in Canada. Your topo map says you'll have to portage your gear around a major falls along the route. The map does not tell you where the portage begins, however. In fact, the *contour lines* (more on this later) suggest there's an impassable canyon wall on both sides of the river.

Want to know more? Then order the aerial photographs from which your map was made. Photos will bring into clear perspective the most obscure features; more so if you specify *stereo pairs.* All you need is an inexpensive stereoscope (available at most hobby shops) to view the land in glorious 3-D. Now, you'll find a route around the falls if one exists!

Note: **Aerial photos are expensive, and they are very large scale (somewhere between 1:24,000 and 1:60,000.) Since there are *millions* of them on file, getting exactly what you want requires *precise* identification of the specific land feature to the nearest 5 minutes of arc.**

For those who don't understand the ways of latitude and longitude: Outline your area of interest on a topo map and send it along with your check to the ESIC or Canada map office. Your map will be returned with your order.

Which Way Is North?

"North," as everyone who has headed "up" north knows, is always at the top of the map. Well, sort of. And for conventional route-finding in the American Midwest, you can get by with that knowledge alone. However, if you plan to travel in the east or west, you'll need to take into account the differences between the *three* norths.

Most important is *true,* or geographical, north. That's the direction in which the lines of longitude run. Since the vertical lines that describe the right and left map margins are true meridians, any line on your map drawn parallel to them runs *true* north and south. Almost!

Meridians converge toward the poles, so the ones that run along your map edges *are not* truly parallel to one another (and the closer you get to each pole, the less parallel they become). No problem; that's what the "neat" lines are for.

Neat lines appear as tiny tick marks at equidistant points along all four map margins. To locate a true north–south meridian, simply connect the neat lines of equal value at the top and bottom of the map (figure 1-6 shows the relationship). Similarly, you can plot a true

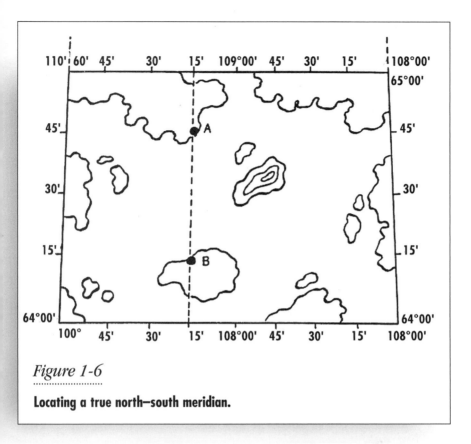

Figure 1-6

Locating a true north–south meridian.

east–west line (parallel) by connecting the latitude neat lines. Then, you can use these coordinates to accurately plot the latitude and longitude of any point on your map.

The Other Norths

Grid north: All topographic maps have *grid lines* imprinted on their faces. Grid lines began life as true meridians and parallels but became distorted when the spherical earth was flattened onto paper. Cartographers use a number of map *projections* to minimize this distortion, but all are subject to some small error. Consequently, grid lines usually *do not* point true north/south or true east/west. The error is reported in a *declination* diagram (refer to figure 4-8, page 47) in the bottom map margin, and is usually small enough that it can be ignored by everyone but surveyors.

Grid north is the north you'll want to use when working with civilian and military topographic maps. Use *true* north with maps that don't have grid lines imprinted on their faces.

Magnetic north: Most everyone knows that the compass needle does not point to true north. Rather, it points toward the north magnetic pole, which is located several hundred miles south of the real thing. The angular difference between the "three norths" is reported in declination diagrams or legend information on all topographic maps. In chapter 4 we'll have a lively discussion of how this affects navigation.

Contour Lines

The thin brown lines on topographic maps are called *contour lines*. They give "depth" and elevation to the land. You'll learn all about them in the next chapter.

Map Symbols

How do you tell (on a map) a school from a church? By the appropriate symbol, of course. There are dozens of map symbols, most of which are obvious. But lest you forget, Canadian maps emblazon them all in the margin or on the back. American USGS maps are more subtle. They tease you with a few road classifications, then assume you know the rest or have on hand their free pamphlet "Topographic Map Symbols," which lists them all.

How Brazen!

You'll find a listing of the most common symbols in appendix I.

Tip: **If you have an old map, don't take the location of trails, unimproved roads, churches, and schools too seriously. It's quite possible that some of these man-made features no longer exist!**

You should also realize that, for clarity, map symbols *are not* drawn to scale—they always appear much larger than they really are. However, the *geometric center* of these symbols is accurately plotted. So shoot a compass bearing (or measure) there if you need to target a particular point.

Easy Map Reading

Understanding Map Contours

The light brown lines overprinted on topographic maps are called *contour lines*. They indicate the elevation above sea level (sometimes, other references are used) of land features and thus permit you to view the topography in three dimensions instead of two. Entire books have been written about contour lines and their interpretation; however, you'll get along quite nicely if you master these basics:

1. Contour lines connect points of *equal* elevation. Thus, closely spaced lines indicate lots of elevation change, whereas widely spaced lines show the opposite (figure 2-1). You gain or lose elevation only when you travel from one contour line to another. If you walk along a contour line, you'll be "on the level."

2. The *contour interval* (CI) is the vertical distance between contour lines. Its value in feet or meters is given in the lower map margin. Thus, if the CI is 50 feet, each successive contour line on the map increases or decreases (as the case may be) in elevation by exactly 50 feet. Each *fifth "index"* contour line is dark colored and is labeled with a number that gives its actual elevation above sea level.

3. The contour interval is determined by the cartographer, based on the amount of elevation change in the area. Mountainous regions will have a contour interval of 50 feet or more, while on relative flatlands it may be 10 feet or less. Consequently, the contour interval *is not* the same for all maps.

Tip: **Convert meters (foreign maps are all metric) to feet (1 meter equals 3.3 feet) if you don't think in the metric system.**

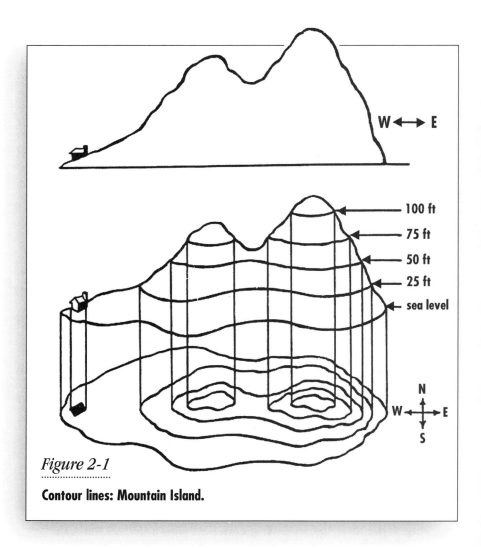

Figure 2-1

Contour lines: Mountain Island.

4. The larger the contour interval, the less clear are the characteristics of the area. In short, a map with a CI of 10 feet gives a clearer picture of the topography than one with a CI of 100 feet. Keep this fact uppermost in your mind when you plan a cross-country hiking or ski trip. Remember, the shortest distance between two points is a straight line only if you're not mountain climbing!

5. Where contour lines cross or run very close together, you'll find an abrupt drop—a falls or canyon (figure 2-2). Especially look for these closely spaced contour lines if you're boating an unknown river. If tight contours *intersect* your route, you can bet there are substantial rapids there.

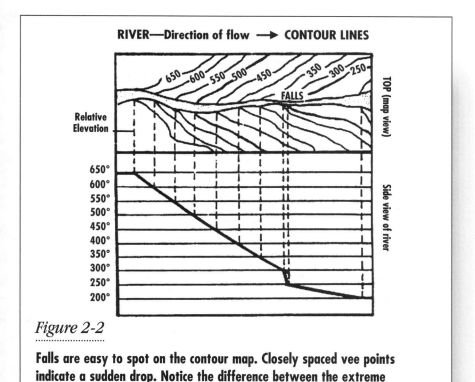

RIVER—Direction of flow ➔ CONTOUR LINES

Relative Elevation

650° 600° 550° 500° 450° 400° 350° 300° 250° 200°

TOP (map view)

Side view of river

Figure 2-2

Falls are easy to spot on the contour map. Closely spaced vee points indicate a sudden drop. Notice the difference between the extreme elevation change at 300'–250' and the long decline between 250'–200'.

To allay your concern, you may want to plot a river *profile* that shows the actual drop per mile.

Making the Profile

Begin by drawing a broad line along each side of the river, parallel to your route. These lines reference your route—and draw your eyes to the river—so you can quickly locate what lies ahead, without visual interference from other map features. I use a translucent felt-tip highlighter pen, the kind college kids prefer for marking important passages in textbooks.

Next, consult the map scale and mark the miles along your route. Gear the number of markers to the map scale. For example, on 1:250,000 maps, I label every 4 miles (figure 2-3), which works out to a mark every inch. On larger-scale maps I tick off each mile. The idea is to clarify without cluttering.

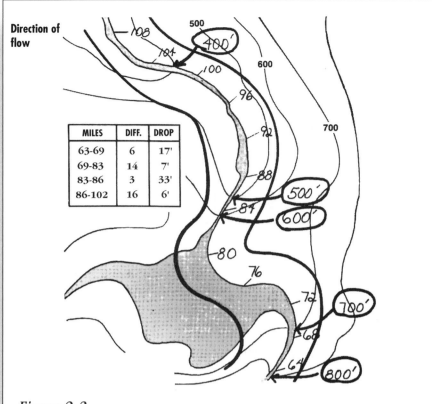

MILES	DIFF.	DROP
63-69	6	17'
69-83	14	7'
83-86	3	33'
86-102	16	6'

Figure 2-3

"The Map Profile" illustrates the techniques used to determine the drop of a typical river. Handwritten circled numbers indicate contours. Distances (miles) are not circled.

Now, get your pencil and draw a small arrow everywhere a contour line crosses the river. Write in the elevations of each contour near the penciled arrow and circle it. Be sure you indicate whether the elevation is in feet or meters.

You're now ready to compute the *drop*. Do the computations in a table similar to that in figure 2-3. For example, the 800-foot contour crosses the river at mile 63, while the 700-foot line intersects at mile 69. This is recorded in the table as *63-69*. The mileage difference is six (69–63). Dividing six into 100 (the value of the contour interval) yields a drop of 17 feet per mile.

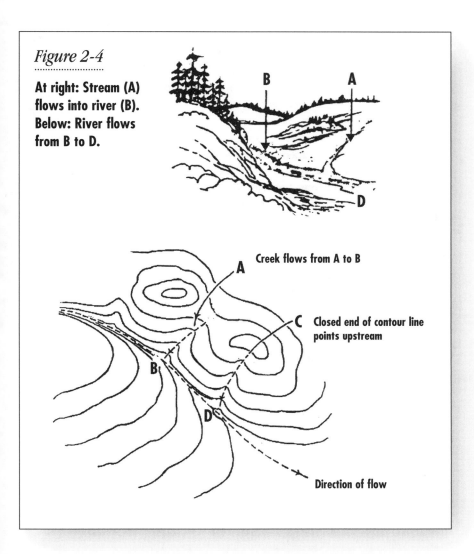

Figure 2-4

At right: Stream (A) flows into river (B). Below: River flows from B to D.

B   A

D

Creek flows from A to B

A

C Closed end of contour line points upstream

B

D

Direction of flow

From mile 69 to 83 the river drops less—7 feet per mile, etc.

In deciding if it's safe to boat an unknown river, keep these rules of thumb in mind:

a. A drop of 3 to 5 feet per mile is nice cruising for an open canoe or fishing boat. 10 feet per mile means gentle rapids. 20 or more is about the limit of an open canoe, and 35 may mean you'll have to portage your rubber raft. *Caution:* These are only guidelines! Maps tell you what to expect—not *what is!* Use your eyes to account for that!

b. Equally important as "drop per mile" is how the drops occur—whether uniformly, or at a falls, dam, or major rapid. Closely spaced drops mean a probable portage at those spots, though the rest of the river may be "user friendly." Uniform drops suggest a wild, fast ride, and your skills had best be up to it!

Note: **You can convert the "top view" of your profile to a side view for greater clarity. Figure 2-2 shows the procedure. You can also use this same method to draw a profile for land masses. Suppose you want to hike cross-country, but a large hill stands in the way. Can you walk the hill, or will you have to crawl up it? To find out the answer, simply draw a line from your location to your destination, and graph the drop as shown in figure 2-2.**

6. The closed or *vee* end of a contour line always points upstream (figures 2-2, 2-4). Note that this rule also applies to creeks, intermittent streams, and gullies.

7. Contour lines become U-shaped (the closed ends of the U's point *downhill*) to indicate the outjutting spur (ridge) of a hill.

8. The actual heights of many objects are given on topographic maps. For example, suppose you find the number 636X printed at a road junction. This means that the X-marked spot is exactly 636 feet above sea level.

Contour Quiz

Use figure 2-5 to test your knowledge of contour lines. Answers are on the next page.

1. Is the creek flowing *into* or *out* of Pikitigushi Lake?

2. You are standing at point (a). What is your height above sea level? (Clue: notice the 1,000-foot contour to the east.)

3. You are standing at point (b), looking towards Pikitigushi Lake. Describe the topography directly in front of you.

4. You are walking south, from (b) to (c). Are you: a) gaining elevation? b) losing elevation? c) remaining level?

5. You walk from (b) to (d). Are you: a) going up a steep hill? b) going down a gully? c) going up a gully?

6. A creek joins lake (e) from the west. Does that creek flow *into* or *out of* lake (e)?

22

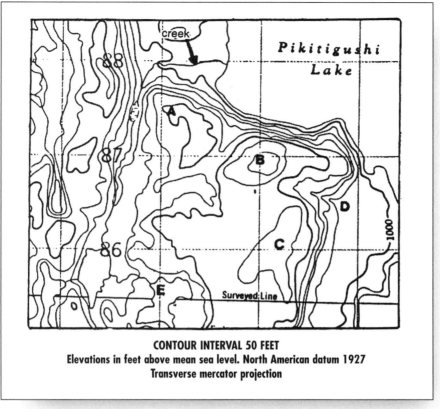

CONTOUR INTERVAL 50 FEET
Elevations in feet above mean sea level. North American datum 1927
Transverse mercator projection

Figure 2-5

Contour quiz illustration.

Answers to Contour Quiz

1. Into the lake. Remember, the closed ends of a contour line point *upstream.*

2. 1,250 feet. The index contour to the east is labeled 1,000. The contour interval is 50 feet; 50 feet x 5 lines = 250 feet of rise.

3. Very steep drop, almost a cliff. You wouldn't want to climb it.

4. You lose 50 feet of elevation (you go down 100 feet to the plateau, then climb 50 feet to reach [c]).

5. (b) Down a gully.

6. The creek flows *to the west,* out of lake "e."

Using the Bar Scale to Measure Horizontal Distances

Most of the time, maintaining map–ground scale relationships is simply a matter of remembering how many inches per mile the scale portrays, and interpolating accordingly. However, sometimes you want a more precise answer than your guesstimate provides. One way is to use the *bar scale* in the map legend, and a piece of scratch paper.

To compute the distance from (a) to (b) in figure 2-6, place the paper edge between the points and transfer this distance to the scale below. You'll get a bit less than three-fourths of a mile.

You can also measure the distance directly with the graduated baseplate of your orienteering compass.

Preparing Your Maps for Use in the Backcountry

Maps are a joy to use if they're well organized and protected from the weather. Here are the recommended procedures:

1. Begin by outlining your route with a felt-tip highlighter. This way you can see where you're going at a glance.

2. If you're hiking or boating on or along a river or lake, you'll want to "tick off" the miles, as explained on pages 19–22, "Making the Profile."

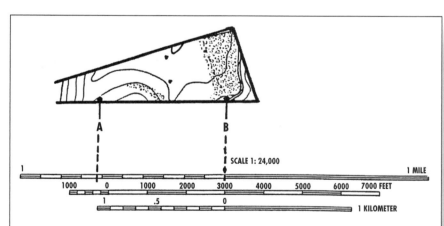

Figure 2-6

....

Mark the location of (a) and (b) on your paper, then compare it to the map bar scale.

This will keep you from biting off more than you can swallow when you do your winter planning. Canoeists, kayakers, and rafters should carefully designate the location of stoppers such as falls and dangerous rapids and the positioning of portage trails. To allay your concern, you may want to draw a river (or trail) profile that shows the actual drop per mile.

3. Maps that will be frequently used in fishing boats are best glued to a thin plywood board, then clear-lacquered to protect them from water. Drill a hole in one corner of the board and attach a nylon security cord. You may also want to tie your compass to the board. Now, everything is at hand and protected from the elements.

Here are some other ways to waterproof your maps:

1. Insert them in Ziploc plastic bags. Giant 12½" x 16" Ziploc bags are available from office supply stores. Camping equipment shops (and most Boy Scout supply centers) carry heavier, similar-sized plastic envelopes with genuine zippers. If you want an inexpensive giant-sized map case, check out your local bait shop. Four-mil-thick "minnow" bags measure 32 x 17½ inches (these are also great for sleeping bags and clothing). Seal the mouth of each bag with duct tape.

2. Cover maps with clear contact paper—it makes them waterproof, but you can't write on them.

3 Paint on Stormproof—a clear chemical that's formulated for use on maps and charts. Most camping shops have it.

4. Apply Thompson's Water Seal—an industrial-strength chemical that's used for sealing concrete blocks. TWS is available in hardware stores in aerosol cans and tins. Apply it with a foam varnish brush. TWS (and Stormproof) makes maps water-repellent, not waterproof. You can write over it with pen or pencil.

5. No sense carrying map portions that you won't use. So trim away unnecessary paper with a scissors before you leave home. If you have a number of map sheets, use either of these methods for organizing them:

   a. Glue the quadrangles together with rubber cement, accurately matching the latitude/longitude neat lines. Cut out important legend information and glue it to the map back or over a nonessential area.

b. Number individual map sheets consecutively. This works fine, except when you find yourself at the edge of a map sheet.

Maps that will be used in the field are better folded than rolled.

Tip: **Discover Forestry Suppliers, Inc., 205 West Rankin Street, Box 8397, Jackson, MS 39204. This company carries a complete line of tools for the professional forester and geologist, including dozens of map aids and laminating films for maps and journals. They carry the complete line of Silva, Suunto, and Brunton compasses. Write for their catalog.**

Anatomy of the Compass

History

No one is certain where or how the compass originated, though it appears that the Chinese were first to discover magnetism in lodestone and its attractive power. One of the first working models consisted of a piece of lodestone floating on a cork in a bowl of water. Other primitive compasses, with magnets shaped like fish or turtles, can be seen in Chinese books that date to the eleventh and twelfth centuries.

The first clear description of a magnetic-needle compass is by Shen Kua, a Chinese, in A.D. 1088—about a century before the earliest mention in European texts. From then on, there are numerous references to compasses in Chinese literature as well as stories about their use by sailors "in dark weather or when the sky is overcast." Other references suggest that primitive compasses were used by Arabian merchants in A.D. 1200 and by Vikings a half century later.

It is not clear whether magnetism and its use for navigation was discovered independently in Europe or brought by travelers from China.

For a while the Chinese led the world in compass production, evidently because the hardened steel needed to hold the magnetism was not available in other parts of the world. But around 1400–1500, Europeans got into the act, and marine compasses became widely available. However, it wasn't until someone realized that compasses could be modified into sundials—and thereby substitute for the expensive watches of the day—that portable field compasses were born.

Little change took place until the end of the pocket sundial period, around 1750. Then came the development of sighting devices and the refinement of the "watch" or "box" compass, which survives today with few modifications.

In the twentieth century we saw substantial improvements in field compasses in the form of the Bezard compass of 1902 and the liquid-filled British Army compass of World War I. But it was not until the 1930s that the real excitement began. First came the development of reasonably-priced, liquid-filled orienteering compasses and birth of the Silva company, then the introduction of protractor-combined plate compasses and sophisticated sighting devices. Things continue on the upswing: The best of today's compasses are a tribute to engineering genius—a quiet lesson in sophisticated simplicity.

Modern Compasses

A half century ago route-finding was a precarious business. Maps of wilderness areas were not always accurate, and compasses were heavy, slow to use, not waterproof, and had no provision for computing bearings from a map.

Now all that has changed. The best modern compasses incorporate complete navigational systems. No longer do you have to grope for a pencil and protractor and "orient the map to north" to take a bearing. And don't let the plastic toylike construction of these instruments fool you. Most of the mid-priced ($15–$25) models can be *consistently* read to within 2 degrees of an optical transit—handheld! Even the cheapies seldom vary by more than 4 degrees.

There are four types of compasses: 1) *fixed-dial* or *standard needle* compass, 2) *floating dial,* 3) *cruiser,* 4) *orienteering.* For hiking, canoeing, hunting, fishing, and just about everything else, only the orienteering type (and where extreme accuracy is required, the floating dial with optical sights) makes much sense. Here are the differences:

Fixed-Dial Compass

Best typified by twenty-five-cent gumball machine models, these "questionably superior" versions of the old "box" compass have degree readings embossed on a fixed outer ring (figure 3-1). The needle rides on a hardened steel or mineral bearing in the center of the capsule. Fixed-dial compasses are slow to use, inaccurate, and not very versatile. People buy them because they don't know how to use any other kind. About all these are good for is zipper pulls on jackets. Nonetheless, because they are so popular, you should know how to use then *effectively.* You'll find the specifics on page 36.

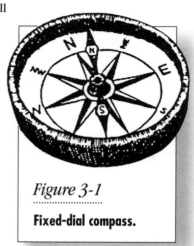

Figure 3-1

Fixed-dial compass.

Floating-Dial Compass

The needle is an integral part of the numbered dial and spins freely on the pivot. You point the compass towards your objective and read the bearing at an index. There's nothing to set, usually, not even a cover to raise. Floating dial compasses run the gauntlet of quality—from five-dollar "hunter pin-on's" to sophisticated direct sighting models like the Suunto KB-14 or the KB-20 (figure 3-2) that can be interpolated to more than 15 minutes of arc.

Cruiser Compasses

These are professional-grade instruments that come in solid metal cases with protective hinged covers, onto which a "lubber's" (sighting) line has been inscribed. Numbers on the dial run counterclockwise (opposite to that of a fixed dial compass) so you can face your objective and the instrument where the north end of the magnetic needle intersects the dial.

Despite their dated design, "cruisers" are still widely used by foresters and geologists. They are accurate, heavy, slow to use, not waterproof, and very expensive.

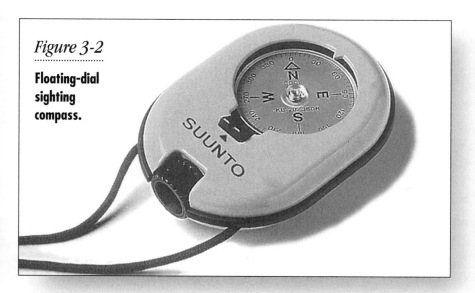

Figure 3-2

Floating-dial sighting compass.

Orienteering Compasses—The Choice of Serious Outdoorspeople

Accuracy is only half the game. The other part is determining what numerical value to set on the compass. For this, you need a map and protractor.

Enter the *orienteering* compass (see figure 3-3). In 1933 Gunnar Tillander, an unemployed instrument worker, approached Björn Kjellstrom and his brothers Alvar and Arvid with a unique plan: Why not incorporate a protractor into the design of a standard needle compass? Almost overnight, the orienteering compass was born. It is unique for these reasons:

1. You can determine bearings from a map *without* the aid of a protractor and without orienting the map to north. This means you can make the computation from the seat of a bobbing canoe or while shuffling down a wilderness trail. You can even do it with mittens on!

2. Your direction-of-travel (bearing) is "locked" onto the compass dial. There's nothing to remember or write down. In fact, you don't even have to read the dial at all!

3. All orienteering compasses have ruled scales along their plastic base plates that make it easy to determine scale distances from a map.

4. Orienteering compasses all have liquid-damped needles. Needle oscillation ceases in three to five seconds. The system works in temperatures down to 40 below zero.

Figure 3-3

A professional orienteering compass.

5. The instrument is so simple that an eight-year-old can learn to run one in a matter of minutes.

For backcountry use, the orienteering compass has no peer. Unless you're running survey lines in search of buried treasure—in which case, you'll want an optical sighting compass—I can think of no reason why you should choose any other kind.

Because the orienteering compass is so versatile, the instruction in this book is centered around its use.

Electronic Digital Compasses

Technology has brought about a number of electronic compasses (see figure 3-4). Some have a memory and chronograph, plus an automatic shut-off switch to save battery drain. A few digital watches feature miniature electronic compasses, though none are accurate or versatile enough for serious navigation.

The best digital compasses are as accurate as the best needle compasses, and their bearings are much easier to read. The bad part is that electronic compasses are powered by batteries, which can fail, and they don't have built-in protractors to obtain map bearings and distances. This rules them out for backcountry use.

Accuracy: How Much Do You Need?

Surveyors and foresters need compasses that give readings to a fraction of a degree. But for general outdoor use, any instrument that will

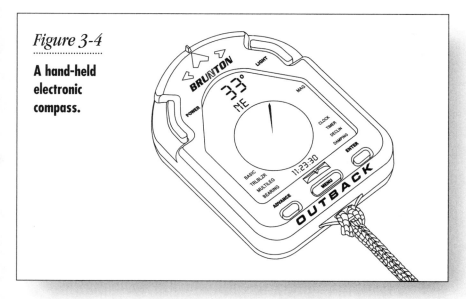

Figure 3-4

A hand-held electronic compass.

consistently read within 4 degrees of a transit will do, even for serious expeditions. You don't need 30-minute accuracy for navigating the back-country. What you do need is a good map and *versatile* compass.

Consider this: One degree of compass error equals 92 feet per mile (tan 1° x 5,280) of ground error. A 4-degree error over a mile course will cause you to miss your objective by 368 feet—hardly significant when you consider *how* compasses are actually used. For example, rather than risk missing their objective (even by 368 feet), experienced travelers "aim-off." That is, they make a purposeful error to the left or right of the reference point. Then, they follow a road, trail, shoreline, powerline, or other "handrail" to their destination. Figure 4-5 in the next chapter details the procedure.

"Aiming-off" becomes even more important when you realize that man-made features such as buildings and trails are frequently misplotted on maps. Under these conditions, clear thinking is more important than precise headings. Here's what you need most in a "working" compass:

1. **Versatility** in transferring bearings from map to ground—hence, the desirability of the orienteering compass.

2. **Speed of operation:** Often, you need to determine a direction from the seat of a bobbing canoe or fishing boat.

3. **Carry ability:** Consider your compass an article of clothing, one you'll wear all the time. The lighter and more compact the instrument, the more pleasurable it will be to carry. Particularly, shun the compass with sharp, square edges. "Square corners" may be great for map plotting, but they'll eat through your clothes in a matter of minutes.

4. **Durability:** I once had a jeep run over an old Silva Ranger. The cover was smashed, but the instrument worked fine. That's tough! A field compass must be built to take everything from a bad fall to a thorough dousing.

5. **Amenities:** Are the scales on the base plate compatible with those on your map? Can the compass be compensated for area magnetic declination? (see chapter 4 for details). Night sights—either luminous or (better) a lithium light—are essential for black night travel. And if you're over age forty, a built-in magnifying glass will clarify map subtleties.

Damping

A compass needle will continue to oscillate for some time unless it is *damped,* either by a light-viscosity liquid *(liquid damping)* or by magnetism *(induction damping)*. Liquid-damped needles stop moving in about three seconds; induction-damped needles take much longer. As to longevity, the vote goes to induction damping, as there's never a chance for a leaky capsule.

However, induction-damped instruments are usually heavier, bulkier, and more expensive than liquid-damped ones. Nearly all the best hand compasses are currently liquid-filled. Except for the Brunton Pocket Transit professional model, induction damping has all but disappeared from the compass scene.

Sights

Some compasses come equipped with sights, which may or may not be a good thing. *Optical* (lensatic and prismatic) sights are most accurate and, in compasses of good quality, give results comparable to expensive surveying instruments.

When you look through an optical sight, you see image, graduated dial, and a vertical intersect line, all in the same plane. The result—in a well-built compass—is accuracy to a fraction of a degree.

Lensatic sights, like those on the old military field compass, are good or bad, depending on the precision of the sight assembly. The original U.S. Army lensatics could be read to 2 degrees of perfection or better. But the ten-dollar foreign copies that currently flood the market are another matter. Most won't read within 5 degrees of a transit!

Combination mirror-vee sight: There's a pop-up mirror with a vertical line scribed through its center. You adjust the mirror to a 60-degree angle (so you can see the alignment of the needle in the capsule), turn your body (not the compass) until the needle is centered within a printed arrow on the dial, then peer across the gunsight vee on the cover top towards your objective. Sounds accurate, and it can be, if you're extremely meticulous. Fact is, you can do as well—often better—by simply holding the instrument waist high and looking straight ahead. Accuracy of the system depends in large measure on precision mounting of the mirror and your ability to keep everything in alignment while holding it all rock-steady.

The problem with *all* nonoptical sights is their very short sighting plane—akin to shooting accurately a pistol with a 2-inch barrel. As explained, the accuracy of any sight depends on the precision and ruggedness of the mounting system. Unfortunately, most hinged compass sights lack the durability for long-term precise alignment. For this reason, your best bet is to use the "waist-high" method of sighting that is explained at the end of this chapter.

Here's what you can expect from the various styles:

Map & Compass   **33**

Compass Type	Probable Maximum Error Without Practice	Probable Maximum Error With Considerable Practice	Approximate Time to Take An Accurate Bearing
Optical sighting	1 degree	½ degree or less	15 seconds
Orienteering	4 degrees	1½ degrees	10 seconds
Induction-damped cruiser	4 degrees	1½ degrees	20 seconds
Liquid-damped fixed-dial	10 degrees	5 degrees	15 seconds

Figure 3-5
....
Characteristics of various compass styles.

Declination

Some compasses have a mechanical adjustment for magnetic declination. This feature is quite inexpensive and is necessary only if you live in an area where declination values are large, or if you are confused by the mathematics of its computation. See the next chapter for details.

Inclination

The earth behaves like a giant magnet, and the closer you get to the poles, the greater the magnetic force. This causes the north end of the needle to tip down in the Northern Hemisphere and to rise in the Southern Hemisphere. Consequently, the compass needle must be balanced for the zone of operation so the needle will spin freely on its pivot.

Professional surveying instruments have a movable counterweight on the needle tail, which can be repositioned if necessary. Field compasses, however, come from the factory balanced for the zone of use. Most any compass you buy in the United States will work fine in North America. Hiking in Ecuador is another matter! Instruments that are balanced for far northern and southern zones are available on special order from the best compass makers.

Dial Graduations

The best compasses have dials that are graduated in 1- or 2-degree increments. Having more graduations than this simply clutters the dial.

However, a lot of fine instruments have 5-degree graduations (especially those with small dials), and this is quite suitable for a field compass.

The rule is that you can interpolate a bearing by twice splitting the distance between the graduations on either side of the index. Thus, a 2-degree dial can be guesstimated to ½ degree; a 5-degree dial to 1¼ degrees, etc. So if you need the most precise readings, opt for finer graduations.

It's important to realize that precision bearings are only useful when combined with optical sighting systems. They are of little value in an orienteering compass. That's because orienteering instruments are almost never "read." Instead, the needle is aligned in the "doghouse" (printed arrow inside the capsule) and the direction-of-travel arrow on the base plate is followed. There is no need to read specific numbers. Indeed, orienteering compasses need not be graduated at all!

How Much Does a Good Compass Cost?

Twenty bucks will buy all the compass you need for wilderness travel. Paying more won't necessarily buy more accuracy or versatility. Options such as declination adjustments, night sights, and sighting devices drive up costs and add little utility. Fact is, the least expensive orienteering models are suitable for the most complex lake and land navigation you're likely to encounter. You *don't* need a professional compass for touring the backcountry.

How to Use the Waist-High Method of Sighting Your Orienteering Compass

Here's the most accurate way to take a bearing to a distant object with an orienteering compass:

Cradle the compass in your right hand and frame the dial with the thumb and forefinger of your left hand (figure 3-6). Forearms should be held gently but firmly against the body to provide a three-point (triangular) position, the apex of which is the compass.

Locate the compass *directly* along the midline of your body, just above your waist and a comfortable distance (about 6 inches) away from your stomach.

Next, turn your body (*not the compass*) until the direction-of-travel arrow on the compass base plate is pointing towards the objective whose bearing you want to determine. Then, while holding the base plate steady, turn the compass housing until the magnetic needle is framed inside the orienting arrow "doghouse" in the clear plastic capsule.

Now, take three "eye-shift" readings to your objective; that is, sight three times from the compass housing to the objective, *without* moving

Read Compass at Index Described on Dial

Figure 3-6

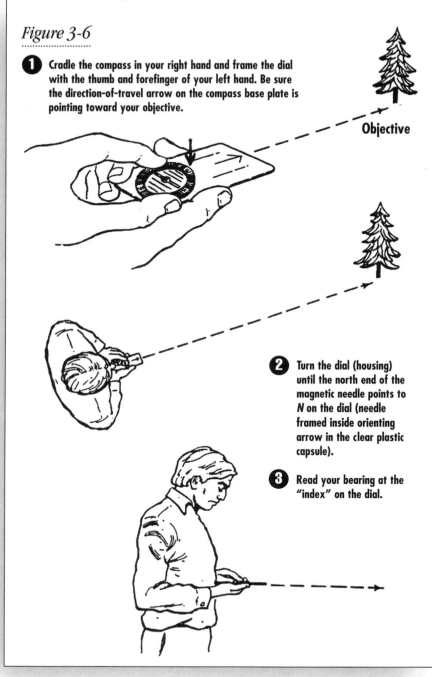

1 Cradle the compass in your right hand and frame the dial with the thumb and forefinger of your left hand. Be sure the direction-of-travel arrow on the compass base plate is pointing toward your objective.

Objective

2 Turn the dial (housing) until the north end of the magnetic needle points to *N* on the dial (needle framed inside orienting arrow in the clear plastic capsule).

3 Read your bearing at the "index" on the dial.

your head. When the alignment of everything—needle in doghouse, direction-of-travel arrow, and objective—is perfect, read your bearing. It should be within 2 degrees of an optical transit.

How to Take an Accurate Bearing with a Fixed-Dial Compass

Although experienced wilderness travelers rely entirely on orienteering-style compasses, they frequently carry a small "gumball machine" compass as an emergency backup. Even a simple "zipper pull" compass can provide accurate directions if you know how to use it. Here's the recommended procedure:

1. Squarely face the objective whose bearing you wish to determine, then frame the compass between your thumbs and forefingers, as illustrated in figure 3-7. Your index fingers form a triangle, the apex of which points to the objective.

2. Rotate the compass between your fingers until the north end of the magnetic needle points to north on the dial.

3. Hold everything rock-steady and read your bearing at the point where your forefingers touch. You should be within 5 degrees of a transit.

Now that you've mastered the workings of map and compass, you're ready to use them together as a complete navigational system. The next chapter shows you how.

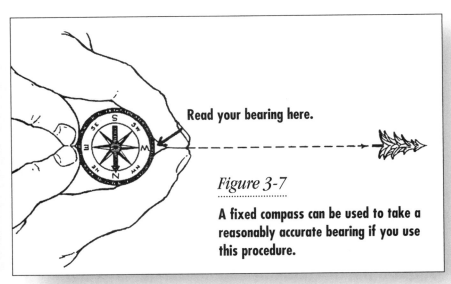

Read your bearing here.

Figure 3-7

A fixed compass can be used to take a reasonably accurate bearing if you use this procedure.

Navigation Basics

First, Some Compass Basics

The compass is graduated in degrees. There are 360 degrees in the compass circle, or *rose* (figure 4-1). The cardinal directions (north, south, east, and west) are each 90 degrees apart. Memorize the eight principal points of the compass and their relationship to the map. This will help eliminate the most common of compass errors—the 180-degree error.

For example: Assume you are fishing Lost Lake (figure 4-2) and are anchored at the peninsula at point E. You want to go to Mud Island,

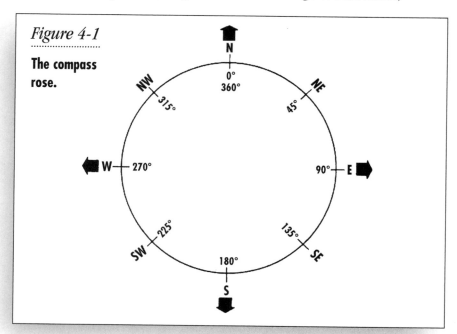

Figure 4-1

The compass rose.

- N — 0° / 360°
- NE — 45°
- E — 90°
- SE — 135°
- S — 180°
- SW — 225°
- W — 270°
- NW — 315°

which lies 1½ miles to the east. With your orienteering compass you inadvertently compute a bearing of 270 degrees, which is 180 degrees in error. However, if you had mentally superimposed the compass rose over point E *before* you determined the map bearing to the island, you'd have instantly discovered your mistake.

It is not uncommon to transfer data from map to compass and make serious directional mistakes. A *knowledge of your approximate direction of travel should be known before you get down to specifics!*

Using the Compass to Determine a Map Bearing

A *bearing* is one of the 360 degree directions of the compass rose. It is always measured *clockwise* from north (either true, grid, or magnetic) to the place you want to go (your objective). For now, we'll forget about the differences between the "three norths" and simply reference our bearing to true north, that is at the top of the Lost Lake map in figure 4-2.

Assume you plan to fish the south end of Long Island, on Lost Lake. That's where the big ones are, or so you've heard! Getting to Long Island from your location at A should be easy: Just head north up the east shoreline, counting bays as you go. When you see Mud Island, hang a left around the north edge and you'll run right into your treasure spot. Easy as pie.

Don't you believe it! Look at the map scale. It's more than 12 miles to Long Island. Even on a clear day, it's doubtful you'll be able to see the intermediate islands or bays along the way. Islands and shoreline will blend to oneness. Because of wind and waves you'll lose all sense of distance traveled. You can easily mistake one of the closer islands for Mud Island, or you can get turned around completely and become convinced that a channel between islands is a large bay, or vice versa.

But getting to Long Island is easy if you have a systematic plan and a compass. The important thing, is to keep track of where you are *all the time*—easy enough if you compute bearings to intermediate checkpoints along the way and reaffirm your position at each point. Here's the procedure:

First, pick a checkpoint on the map. It should be some place that's reasonably close and easily identifiable—a small island, the tip of a peninsula, a prominent bay, etc. You may or may not be able to see these checkpoints (or *attack points,* as they're called in orienteering terms) from your location at A.

You decide that your first attack point will be the southern tip of Horseshoe Island, 2¾ miles away. Begin by guesstimating the bearing from your location at A to your objective at B. You'll be heading *northwest,* or about 315 degrees. Remember that number!

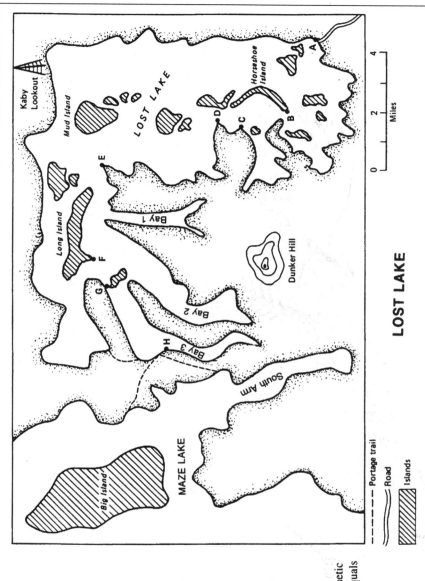

Figure 4-2

Lost Lake Practice Map.

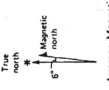

True north

Magnetic north

6°

Average Magnetic Declination Equals 6 East.

LOST LAKE

Next, determine the actual compass bearing from A to B, with your orienteering compass (preferred) or a protractor.

Protractor Method

Use this if you *don't* have an orienteering compass.

1. Draw a line from A to B.

2. Center your protractor over A and align "protractor north" with true north on your map (figure 4-3). Remember, true north is at the *top* of your map. Its direction is indicated by the starred leg of the declination diagram (more on this later) in the right map margin.

3. Read the protractor at the line intersect. You get 290 degrees.

4. Compare this figure (290 degrees) with your guesstimate of 315 degrees. Are the two within 90 degrees of one another? Good. You haven't made an error: You *know* you're going in the right direction!

Computing the Bearing with an Orienteering Compass

1. Place either the left or right edge of the compass base plate over point A. Place the forward edge of the *same* side of the base plate on point B. Your compass is now pointing in the direction you want to go—*from A to B,* not from B to A (figure 4-4).

2. *While holding the base plate tightly in position,* turn the compass housing until north on the dial points to the top (true north) of the map. *Caution:* Don't use the magnetic needle! Your direction of travel—290 degrees—is now locked onto the dial and can be read at the index inscribed on the compass base.

3. Now . . . while holding the compass in front of you with the direction-of-travel arrow inscribed on the base pointing away from your body, rotate your body with the compass until the magnetic needle points to north on the dial. Look straight ahead. You are now facing 290 degrees—toward Horseshoe Island.

4. All that's necessary now is to locate a notch or visible incongruity on the horizon that you can identify as being on this course of travel. Put your compass away, fire up your motor, and cruise toward your objective.

Note: **This is identical to the waist-high sighting method described on page 36, except that instead of shooting a bearing to a distant point, you're computing it from a map.**

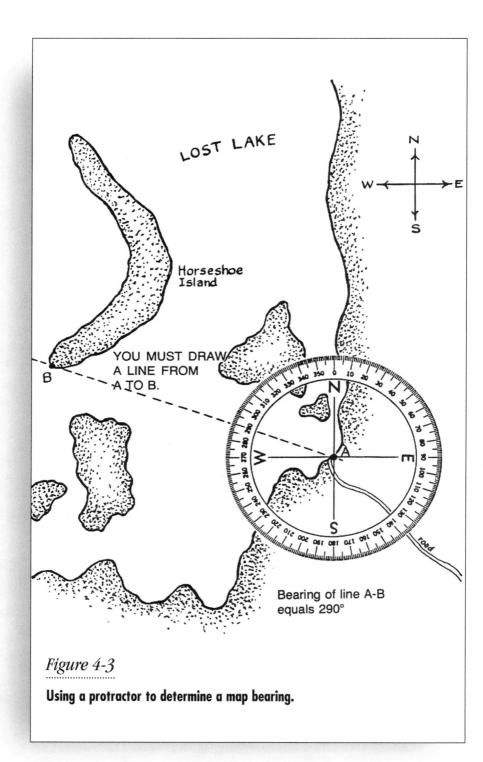

LOST LAKE

Horseshoe
Island

YOU MUST DRAW
A LINE FROM
A TO B.

B

Bearing of line A-B
equals 290°

Figure 4-3

Using a protractor to determine a map bearing.

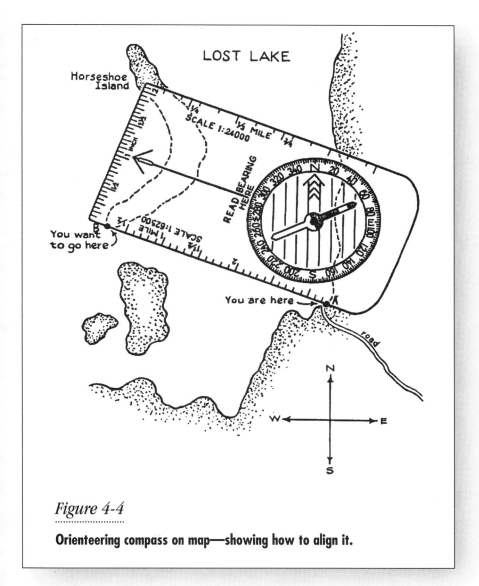

Figure 4-4

Orienteering compass on map—showing how to align it.

Okay, test time. Use your orienteering compass or protractor to compute the true bearings from points A through G on the Lost Lake map. Check your answers on page 44. Don't try to compute distance, travel time, or magnetic bearing. We'll get to these later.

Answers to Lost Lake Exercise

Point	True bearing	Distance (miles)	Approximate travel time	Magnetic bearing (to be set on your compass)
A to B	290°	2¾	1½ hours	284°
B to C	341°	1½	¾ hour	335°
C to D	15°	⅘	20 minutes	9°
D to E	338°	4	2 hours	332°
E to F	274°	3¼	1½ hours	268°
F to G	244°	1⅛	½ hour	238°
G to H	227°	2½	1¼ –1½ hours	221°

H to portage (paddle north up the shoreline to portage): Time—about 15 minutes.

Aiming Off

Proceeding from attack point to attack point is as useful on land as it is on water, with one exception: Trees! Getting around them necessarily means reestablishing your bearing after every "run in"—not impossible, but awkward enough to preclude pinpoint targeting of your objective. For this reason, precise compass bearings are usually modified by *aiming off.* This simple procedure ensures you'll hit your objective head-on. Consider the following scenario.

You've parked your car at point A in figure 4-5 and have hiked the trail to McClaren Lake (point B). You may take any one of the three routes on the return leg. You can hike the trail back to A—a weaving, time-consuming route, though one on which you can't possibly get confused. You can follow the trail to its end at Goldbar Lake (C), then continue on down the creek to the road at D and from here, walk 1½ miles east to your car.

But wait! Look at the topography between C and D. The value of each contour line, in feet, is labeled and circled on the map, and the contour interval, as given in the map legend, is 50 feet. Arrows mark where each contour crosses the creek. As you can see, the creek drops 300 feet (1,000 minus 700) in the 1½-mile distance from Goldbar Lake to the road, and likely, it's all through a tangle of head-high brush. Working your way down this steep slope, climbing over downed trees and tag alder, might take much longer—and be far more unpleasant—than backtracking over the trail.

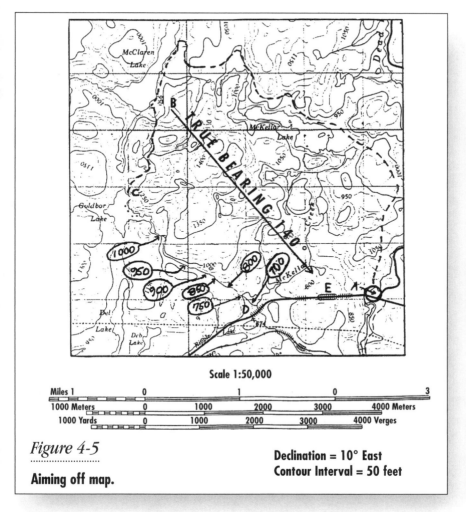

Figure 4-5
....
Aiming off map.

Declination = 10° East
Contour Interval = 50 feet

There's an alternative, however—a straight compass shot from B to A. You'll be going overland, so it'll be tough sledding. And you'll have to avoid the scattered ponds and wade a few creeks. But it will spell adventure—the reason why you came here in the first place. And it would be awesomely remote. If you use your compass, you won't get lost.

Let's do it! Here's the procedure.

If you compute a direct bearing from your present location at B, to A, your chance of arriving on target at the road junction is very small. After all, you'll be climbing up and down hills, skirting ponds and brush piles. That you won't be able to maintain a precise course over this rough ground is a forgone fact. Better to compensate for this error by aiming off a bit to the west—say to point E. Granted, you'll probably miss E, but you *will* strike the road somewhere east or west of it. Once you hit the road just follow it east to your starting point. Simple, isn't it?

If aiming off is useful on land, it's even more useful on water. For example: Suppose you're located at point G on the Lost Lake map (figure 4-2). You want to take the portage trail that leads to the South Arm of Maze Lake, just north of H. There are three portages leading out of Bay 3, but only one goes to South Arm. From G to the South Arm trail is about 3 miles. A 4-degree error over this distance would cause you to miss your objective by at least 1,100 feet (remember, 1 degree of compass error equals 92 feet per mile of ground error), or nearly a quarter mile—enough to send you scurrying down the wrong trail.

The solution is to aim off to H—an unidentifiable point just south of the trail. Then, when you reach the shoreline, turn right (north). The first path you come to is the right one.

Declination

A compass points (actually, it doesn't point—it lines up with the earth's magnetic field) to *magnetic* north, not *true* north. This angular difference, called *declination,* must be considered whenever you use your compass (figures 4-6, 4-7). In the eastern United States the declination is westerly; in the western United States it's easterly. If you live right on the imaginary line that goes directly through both the true and magnetic north poles (called the *agonic* line), your declination will be zero.

On the other hand, if you live east or west of the agonic line, your compass will be in error, since the true north pole is not in the same

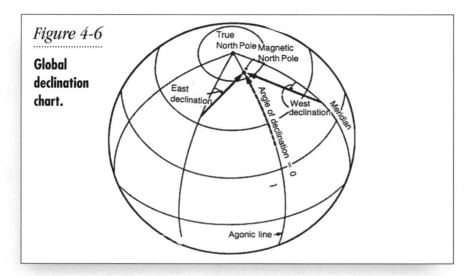

Figure 4-6

Global declination chart.

True North Pole
Magnetic North Pole
East declination
West declination
Angle of declination = 0
Meridian
Agonic line →

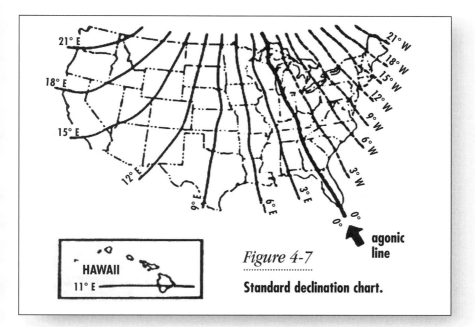

Figure 4-7

Standard declination chart.

place as the magnetic north pole. As you can see from the declination chart, the farther away you are from the agonic line, the greater the declination. Moreover, the magnetic pole is constantly moving; because of this, declination will vary from year to year as well as place to place. Consequently, it's not possible for compass makers to factory-adjust a compass to account for this variation.

To find the exact declination for your area, consult your topographic map. You'll find the declination value in a diagram in the lower map margin. It will look something like this:

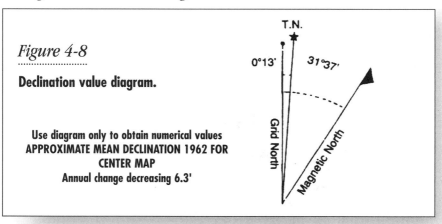

Figure 4-8

Declination value diagram.

Use diagram only to obtain numerical values
APPROXIMATE MEAN DECLINATION 1962 FOR
CENTER MAP
Annual change decreasing 6.3'

Note that the "legs" of the declination diagram in figure 4-8 *are not* drawn to angular scale (some diagrams *are*). The angles are slightly exaggerated for clarity—a note to that effect appears in the legend. Consequently, you shouldn't use the direction of the magnetic flag as an accurate pointing for your compass. Instead, adjust the instrument mathematically, as explained in the following section.

1. The star (★) indicates the direction of true north. This leg of the diagram runs parallel to a line of longitude.

2. The flag (▲) points to magnetic north. If the flag is to the right (east) of the north star, the area declination is east. If it's to the left of the star, the declination is west.

3. The black sphere (●) indicates the direction of the grid lines on the map. *Remember:* Topographic maps do not have lines of longitude imprinted on their faces, but they do have grid lines. The two *are not* the same! When you peel the skin off a globe (earth) and lay it flat, you distort the curved meridians. This distortion—or variation from true north—is reported in all declination diagrams.

Interpreting the Diagram

In figure 4-8, grid north is 13 minutes west of true north.

Magnetic north is 31°24' (31°37'-0°13') east of true north (you should round it off to 31 degrees). This is the direction your compass needle will point. It is also the value of the *declination,* that is defined as the *angle between true north and magnetic north.*

You can also determine *grid declination* from the diagram. It is the angle between *grid north* and magnetic north—in this case, 31°37' east, or 32 degrees when rounded off. The section on grid declination on page 50 tells you how to use this important figure.

Dealing with Declination

Check out the declination on the Lost Lake map (figure 4-9) on page 49. It equals 6 degrees east. There are no grid lines on this map, hence, no need to identify *"grid"* north.

As stated, maps are almost always drawn in their true perspective (any variation here is so small it can be ignored). So any bearing you determine *from the map* by using the top of the map or the east or west border (line of longitude) as a north reference, is, by definition, a *true* bearing. The bearings you computed in the A-through-G "point-to-point" exercise were therefore all true bearings. *Now, you must change these true values to magnetic ones that will be set on your compass*

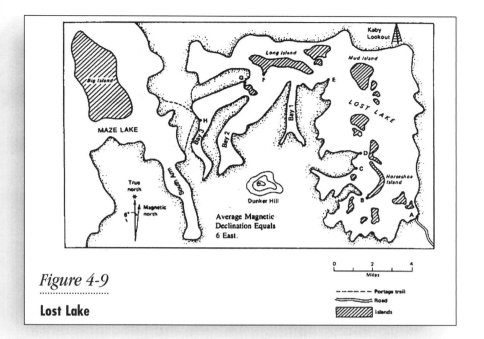

Figure 4-9

Lost Lake

and followed on the ground—easy enough, if you remember the simple rhyme:

Declination east—compass least
(subtract east declination from your map direction).
Declination west—compass best
(add west declination to your map direction).

Your true bearing from A to B in the Lost Lake exercise was 290 degrees. Change it to a magnetic bearing by application of the rhyme. *Subtract* six degrees and you get 284. Adjust your compass for this new heading and take off. You'll hit point B head-on.

Conversely, if the declination were west, you would add its value (290 + 6 = 296) to your compass reading.

Note: **It makes no difference in which direction (north, south, east, or west, or something in between) you are going on the map sheet. If the declination is east, you always subtract its value from your true map bearing. If it's west, you add it. If this is confusing, you may want to buy a compass that can be adjusted for declination.**

Okay, test time … again. Convert all your *true* Lost Lake bearings to *magnetic* ones. Answers are on page 44.

Map & Compass   49

Grid Declination
....

Grid lines take the guesswork out of aligning your protractor or orienteering compass to map north. Remember, however, that *grid lines don't point true north,* so you'll have to compensate for their variation.

Any bearing you compute off a map, using *grid north* (any grid line) as the north reference line is, by definition, a *grid bearing.* Before you can follow this bearing on the ground, you must first convert it to a *magnetic bearing* by application of the "east is least, west is best" rhyme.

The grid declination in figure 4-8 (page 47) is 31°37' east, or 32 degrees, when rounded off. Subtract 32 degrees from your grid bearing and set this value on your compass. That's all there is to it. The procedure is identical to that used to change a true bearing to a magnetic one.

In truth, we're splitting hairs here, for grid north is so close to true north (just 13 minutes away) that the difference is meaningless. This isn't always the case, however, so check out the values before you commit to your *accurate* field bearings. Admittedly, true and grid north seldom vary by much more than 3 degrees, so for typical field use the two can usually be considered as one.

Tape Method of Adjusting the Compass for Declination

If you don't want to mess with the mechanics of adding or subtracting declination values from your true or grid bearings, you can adjust your compass to compensate. Here's how.

Given: You have computed a *true* map bearing of 60 degrees to your objective. The area declination is 10 degrees east.

Procedure: Place a narrow piece of tape across the face of the compass housing so that it goes over the needle pivot and intersects both the 10-degree and 190-degree marks. Your compass is now adjusted to compensate for a 10-degree east declination.

Now . . . hold the compass in front of you and find the bearing on the ground—only *don't* frame the magnetic needle in the doghouse (printed arrow in the capsule) as is customary. Instead, align it with the tape mark, which is 10 degrees east of north. Note that you are actually facing a bearing of 50 (60 degrees minus 10 degrees).

Conversely, if the declination were 10 degrees west, you would apply the tape so that it intersected the 350-degree (that's 10 degrees west) and 170-degree marks. As you might guess, the mechanical declination adjustments on sophisticated compasses use this very procedure.

Adjusting Your Map for Declination

You can also adjust your map for declination by drawing lines that run parallel to the north magnetic pole, across its face. Then, when you compute map headings, just align the printed arrow in the capsule of your orienteering compass with these lines, rather than "map north" (top of the map). All competitive orienteering maps are set up like this. However, the system works much better with small orienteering maps than with 2½-foot-square topos. Try drawing parallel lines across a standard-sized topographic map and you'll see why. Best stick with a more conventional treatment of declination.

Updating the Declination

The magnetic poles are constantly moving. Their location changes from year to year (and from minute to minute). Movements are subtle, however—generally small enough that only surveyors interested in extreme accuracy need worry about them.

The problem only surfaces when you're working off a very old map. For example, the legend in figure 4-8 states (page 47) "APPROXIMATE MEAN DECLINATION 1962 . . . annual change decreasing 6.3'."

This means that magnetic north (the flag) is moving *westward* (decreasing) by 6.3 minutes per year. Updating the declination is easy:

1. Determine the elapsed years (2001 - 1962 = 39 years).

2. Multiply the annual change by the elapsed years (6.3' x 39 years) = 245.7 minutes.

3. Convert minutes to whole degrees (245.7 ÷ 60 = 4.09 . . . or 4 degrees.

4. Subtract this figure from the 1962 declination of 31 degrees (31° – 4° = 27°). Your declination for 2001 is 27 degrees east.

Note: **To update the grid declination, merely subtract 4 degrees from the grid magnetic angle of 32 degrees. Answer: 28 degrees east.**

Position by Triangulation

Suppose you're lost on a large, maze-like lake, but you can recognize two or more topographical features off in the distance. Use your orienteering compass (or protractor and conventional compass) to find

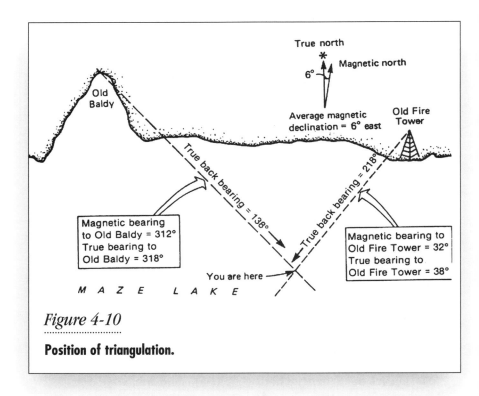

Figure 4-10

Position of triangulation.

your position by *triangulation.*

Pick out one point on the horizon that you can identify—Old Baldy, in this case (see figure 4-10). Shoot a magnetic bearing to the point (bearing = 312 degrees). Change this magnetic bearing to a true bearing by reverse application of the rhyme: $312° + 6° = 318°$. Draw the back (reciprocal) bearing ($318° - 180° = 138°$) through Old Baldy, using your compass base plate and a sharp pencil.

Tip: **When using an orienteering compass you don't have to compute the back bearing at all. Simply set 318 degrees on the compass dial, place your pencil point on Old Baldy, and put the forward edge of one side of the base plate against the pencil point. Rotate the entire compass in an arc about the pencil until north on the dial (not the needle) points to the top (true north) of the map.** *Caution:* **Do not turn the compass housing during this operation, since the true bearing that you just computed to Old Baldy (318°) is set on the dial. This procedure will not work if you change the dial setting!**

Now ... using the base plate as a straight edge, draw your line. Repeat the exercise using another point that you can identify (the old fire tower). You are located where the two lines cross.

Okay, now for another test, using the Lost Lake map. You can identify Dunker Hill at a magnetic bearing of 253 degrees and Kaby Lookout at a magnetic bearing of 4 degrees. Where are you located? *Clue:* Don't forget to apply the declination. You'll find the answer on page 54.

Relocating a Good Fishing Spot by Triangulation

You don't need to identify points on a map to use triangulation. In fact, you don't need a map at all! Suppose you've discovered a real hot spot—the fish are biting like crazy. You definitely want to come here again! Problem is, there are no identifying landmarks to guide the way. And the fishing hole is small, just a dozen yards in diameter. How on earth will you find this place again?

Easy! Just shoot compass bearings to two or more places on the shoreline. The tall pine on the right (figure 4-11) and broken-down cabin at left are ideal. But your points need not be so sophisticated. A moss-covered boulder or leaning tree will do. Anything that won't "run off" will work. Since you don't have a map, there's no need to compute back bearings, or to draw intersecting lines. Instead, simply record the

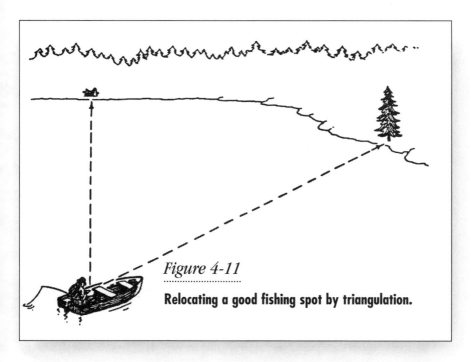

Figure 4-11

Relocating a good fishing spot by triangulation.

numbers in a notebook for future reference. Next time you come here, look for the cabin and pine tree. Then, position yourself where the two bearings match.

Free Triangulation

This is the same as two-point triangulation, except you need just one reference line. Assume you're hiking along the railroad track in figure 4-12 and want to establish your exact position. In the distance you see a large hill that stands out boldly among the flatlands. You shoot a compass bearing to the hill and get 156 degrees.

Convert this *magnetic* reading to *true* direction by reverse application of the rhyme: 156° + 10° = 166°. Next, determine the *back bearing* (166° + 180° = 346°) and plot it on the map. You're located where the line crosses the track.

Use free triangulation any place you can establish a single line of reference—a road, trail, river, creek, lakeshore, or power line.

Answer to triangulation problem: You are located at the north end of Horseshoe Island.

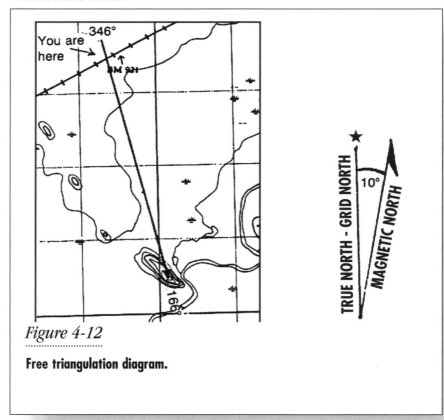

Figure 4-12

Free triangulation diagram.

Tricks of the Trade

I f you've progressed this far, you're just short of being expert with map and compass. You can now compute map bearings, convert them to magnetic readings, and chart a course through tangled brush or the maze of islands on a fog-bound lake. You know all about aiming off, triangulation, and declination plus a wealth of other navigation procedures.

So congratulations on your hard-earned confidence. You're almost ready to cope with the worst of times on the best of terms. What you need now is practice, practice, practice ... plus a working knowledge of some tricks of the trade. Here are a few.

Outdoor books are rich with tales of men who traveled the haunting wilds with only the stars or a simple compass to guide them. Of course, it *can* be done and has been done, but the risks of injury are very real.

However, night travel takes on new dimensions if the sky is gentle gray or if you have a full moon or powerful headlamp to guide the way. And oh yes, don't rely on luminous compass points to keep you on track. Compass "night sights" are very primitive: Without frequent light to recharge their chemical batteries, they fail. None will last the night. A flashlight—or other light source—is essential.

Problem: **Calculate the distance between points on the Lost Lake practice map in chapter 4. Assume a travel speed of 2 miles per hour. Check your answers on page 44.**

As to navigation by the stars (discounting *celestial* navigation, of course), I know of no one who has ever had to resort to such folly. If you are lost or without a compass, you have no business traveling at night, and if you do have a compass you certainly don't need the stars. Moreover, trees and topographical features sometimes prevent you from keeping the North Star in view. Such star navigation makes interesting reading, but it's impractical. However, if you're interested in this sort of thing, check out a Boy Scout handbook or standard text on surveying.

Navigation at Night

Over the years I've done a fair amount of black night canoe travel on large sprawling lakes. Most memorable was the time I camped in the Boundary Waters Canoe Area of Minnesota and was awakened to find three bears merrily munching dehydrated prunes that my teen group had carelessly thrown about. We blew whistles, clanged pans, and yelled loudly. No luck. The bruins remained oblivious to the racket and kept right on eating.

When they knocked down one tent, we decided it was time to leave. Within minutes we struck camp and put to sea. There was no moon or stars; just full cloud cover and vast nothingness. Visibility was a flat zero.

Fortunately, I had a flashlight and my Silva Ranger compass. I carefully plotted a beeline for a distant island that had a campsite. Then I set the compass on the floor of my canoe and unerringly kept the luminous point on the magnetic needle aligned with the glowing aid dots that flanked it.

Before we dipped paddles, I carefully computed the distance from our location to the island. It was almost exactly 3 miles. At an approximate paddling speed of 2 cautious miles per hour, we should arrive on target in ninety minutes. I set my watch alarm and peeled out into the blackness of the night.

Exactly eighty minutes later, we touched shore. There was the island ... and the welcome campsite.

Moral: You need more than good bearings for black night travel. You also need to keep track of your distance and time!

Traveling overland on a dead dark night is another matter. Some years ago, as a forester with the Bureau of Land Management in Oregon, I was lost for three days in the mountains south of Coos Bay. Again, I had my trusty Silva, but this time, no map. Referencing was a "matter of the mind": I knew Highway 101 was about 60 miles due west. I tried to travel the first night, but it was no use. After a number of life-threatening falls, I gave up in disgust and waited till sunrise.

Around noon of the third day, I struck a logging road and the sound of a clanging diesel tractor. Humility? You bet. When I returned to work the next day, I never told a soul. After all ... foresters don't get lost!

— Cliff Jacobson

River Navigation

Everything in this book has been necessarily centered around land and lake navigation. After all, that's where you'll be navigating most of the time. But suppose you want to canoe or raft a wild, brawny river. Are there navigational concerns other than those mentioned in chapter 2?

You bet! With the impact of man on river systems, it is becoming more and more important for river users to know what the water conditions are before they go afloat. Many local and even far northern rivers are now dam-controlled and are very dangerous at high water or impossible during the "walking levels" of late summer. Barbed-wire fences strung across rivers maim and kill boaters each year, and the people who string these fences usually have the law on their side. Each year, we read about canoeists and fishermen who inadvertently paddled over a dam because they didn't know it was there.

If you boat rivers, you must be able to accurately locate and identify dams, rapids, fences, and other obstacles that can endanger your trip. The symbols for many of these appear on your topographic map, but not all. And frequently what's there is incorrect. Here are some ways to outfox the inadequacies of your map.

1. Continually check the *level* of the tree line as you paddle along. If tree heights fall off suddenly, there's a dam or falls ahead.

2. Maps do not indicate obstacles that are the result of river turbulence. Waves pile up on the *outside* of bends, and so does debris. Except in very low water, you should always stay on the *inside* curves of a river.

3. It is very difficult to fix your position on a river. A compass will be useful for rough directions only. Of course, you can reaffirm your location at major bends, rapids, or incoming streams, or you may be fortunate enough to locate an identifiable object upon which you can plot a line of free triangulation.

Lastly, some of the best sources of river conditions are the people who live in the area. Always check with them before embarking on a river, even if you've run it many times. Be aware, however, that locals tend to exaggerate the dangers of their river. So especially seek out foresters or professional people who work in the area. Outdoors people will generally tell it like it is . . . or at least they'll exaggerate less.

And if one day your dreams take you to the far north, where rivers run cold and help is an airplane ride away, you'll need to know (*absolutely know!*) your precise location at all times. Contrary to what you may have read or heard, compasses are generally quite reliable near the Arctic Circle—that is, if you can correctly apply the declination— which may change with each few miles you travel!

Navigating Streams and Moose Trails

Finding your way through a maze of beaver streams and moose trails calls for resourcefulness. Remember, modern maps are made from aerial photos, and if you can't see the sky because of a dense tree canopy or tall grass, the plane-mounted camera can't see the stream. Therefore, your map may be in error in these places, though the general flow of the water course—minus the switchbacks—is usually accurate.

The heads and mouths of small streams are almost always plotted correctly, but deciphering the maze in between often calls for a ready compass. Moreover, stream beds are constantly changing, and these changes will not be reflected on a topographic map that is many years old.

Some hints for navigating small meandering streams: 1) Where a stream forks, take the route with the strongest flow, even if it looks more restrictive than a broader channel. If there is no discernible current, note which way the grass bends in the channel and follow; 2) Check your compass frequently— don't rely on your map, especially if it is many years old; 3) If you come to a dead end and see a portage trail, scout it before you carry your canoe or boat across. Your "portage" may simply be a heavily used animal trail that leads to a connecting tributary or a dead-end pond.

Your Watch as a Compass

Although of questionable accuracy, direction finding using a watch is at times convenient when you want a rough, quick direction but you don't want to get out your compass. If your watch is correctly set for the time zone in which you're traveling, just hold the watch horizontal and point the hour hand at the sun. Half-way between the hour hand and twelve o'clock (see figure 5-1) is south. Such showmanship will impress your friends when things get dull on a long trip

By the way, you can also use your compass as a watch. Just keep in mind the hourly positions of the sun, which are

6:00 A.M.—*east* 3:00 P.M.—*southwest*
9:00 A.M.—*southeast* 6:00 P.M.—*west*
NOON—*south*

Using the Stars as a Compass

Follow the two "pointer" stars on the cup of the Big Dipper to the North Star (Polaris), which is the tail star of the Little Dipper (figure 5-2, page 60). The Dippers are "circumpolar" constellations, so they're visible all year round from any place in the Northern Hemisphere. Polaris is seldom more than one degree east or west of true north.

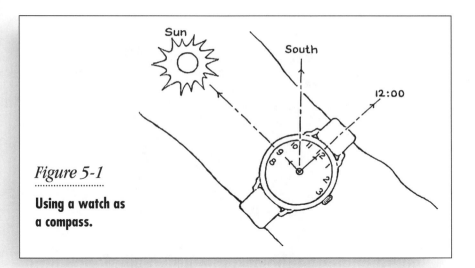

Figure 5-1
....
Using a watch as a compass.

To Determine Declination by the Stars

If your map does not provide magnetic declination information, drive two pointed sticks into the ground and line them up with the North Star, as illustrated in figure 5-3. The longer stick should be "north" of the shorter stick. The angle between the compass needle and true north is the magnetic declination of your area. Be sure to note whether the declination is east or west! Naturally, this procedure works best when declination angles are very large.

Baselines

Most every book on wilderness navigation has a chapter devoted to "the lost hunter"—relocating your remote camp, finding the remains of the deer you shot, etc. But it's all simply a matter of baselines, that is, you establish a reliable handrail (road, stream, powerline, etc.) Then use it as a reference line for your bearings. Figure 1-1 is a typical example of this relationship—one which again proves the importance of a map. Note, however, that you don't need a formal map to travel the backwoods with confidence. A mind relationship is often enough.

There's no substitute for common sense. To this add a good map and a compass and a practiced hand, and you'll have all the tools you need to confidently navigate the backcountry.

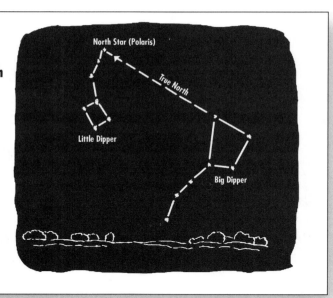

Figure 5-2

How to tell north by using the stars.

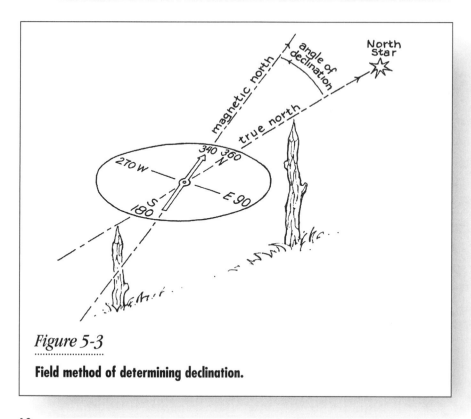

Figure 5-3

Field method of determining declination.

Shadow Sticks

No one should set out into unfamiliar territory without a compass. However, if you happen to be stranded in a polar region or in an exceptionally ore-rich territory where compasses don't work properly, or if your compass is lost or damaged, there are still several ways of determining the proper direction.

First, as most everyone knows, the sun rises in the east and sets in the west. But it neither rises in a due east direction or sets in a true west direction except in certain areas. In fact, in the far north the position of the sun can be very misleading, and so the stick-and-shadow method (Figure 5-4, page 63)) should be used to plot due east and west. Furthermore the stick-and-shadow method can sometimes be used on cloudy days when the sun isn't visible because even on a cloudy day the sun might cast a shadow. (The moon also can be used if it is bright enough to cast a shadow.)

First cut a stick at least 3 feet long and stick it upright in the ground where the ground is flat and bare of vegetation. Then cut two marker sticks, each about 1 foot long, and stick one in the ground at the tip of the shadow cast by the 3-foot stick. About ½ hour later drive the second stick into the ground at the tip of the shadow again. It will have moved from the first mark. Now cut a direction pointer stick, sharpen one end, and lay it against the two marker sticks with the sharp end against the second marker stick. The sharpened end will point east and the blunt end will point west. This will be true anywhere in the world, since the sun always moves in an east to west path.

Now having marked true east and west, align your body with the direction stick so your extended right arm will point east and your left arm directly west. Now you will be facing north. With all four directions found, you can plot your travel path from them.

Actually, shadows from natural objects roughly indicate directions whenever you know the approximate time. In early morning, they should lay nearly west; at mid-morning, northwest; at noon, north; mid-afternoon, northeast; and at sunset, east.

Night Sights

Any bright star can be used for plotting directions: Drive a stick in the ground and then back off about 10 feet and drive another in the ground so you can sight across the top of the two sticks at the star (see Figure 5-5, page 64). If you watch the star for several minutes across the tops of the stick, it will either rise, fall, or swing to the left or to the right. If it falls you are looking west, if it is rising you are sighted toward the east. If it swings toward the left you are looking north. Swinging toward the right indicates south. But you only have to remember that a rising star

A Lifesaving Compass

Recently near a small town in upper Michigan, a couple stopped at a motel. It was early in the afternoon and the elderly lady decided to go for a walk. She never returned. Weeks later a search party found her body beside a wooded road about 12 miles from the motel.

Even though it was summer, hypothermia set in after dark and she expired. Yet if she had known the right direction, she could have walked to help in a half hour.

We live on the edge of a large expanse of forest, and several times lost deer hunters have followed the light to our cabin after they got lost. Some are seasoned outdoorspeople. Most times they have no idea where their vehicle is, and even after I find it for them, they are so disoriented they don't know the way back to town until I tell them. Usually they are on the verge of exhaustion, and in the Wisconsin northwoods in winter, an exhausted human might not last until morning.

I get turned around about as often as anyone, and always have. But because I know I have this weakness, I have trained myself to react wisely when I discover I am not walking in the right direction. One good example happened during a western hunting trip.

I was tracking an elk on a mountainside near Pinedale, Wyoming, when I finally lost track of the herd. Then I realized that the peak I had absently been looking at for some time was not the peak I thought it was.

I remember feeling in my pocket for the compass and the great feeling of utter joy and relief that came over me when my groping fingers touched it. With compass in hand, I plotted a course. At first I was tempted to walk due north, hoping to hit the horse trail. But I changed my mind when I realized how easy it would be to walk right beside the trail and never know it was there. I decided instead to walk east to a large burned-over area, follow its edge to the north side of the peak, and then walk west to the horse trail.

I had barely started walking when it began snowing heavily, almost blotting out the landscape. With no sun to guide me, the compass literally became a lifesaving device. At that I didn't reach the trail until just before dark. I could have easily died on that peak that night, because after it stopped snowing it turned bitterly cold. The compass literally saved me.

—James Churchill

indicates east, and a star moving toward your left hand will indicate you are sighting across the sticks in a northerly direction, since the other two directions are opposite.

Hints from Habitat

After you find the right direction to travel, by the position of the sun, stars, or moon, study the vegetation and topography to see if they contain clues to the four directions. Then, if the next travel day is cloudy, take your clues from the surrounding habitat. In many regions the prevailing westerly winds will shape shrubs and small trees so they lean in an easterly direction. Watersheds will follow a certain direction, and rivers and major streams will flow in one direction. Sand dunes and snowdrifts will be shaped by the prevailing winds into repetitive patterns that will indicate directions.

South slopes will probably have different vegetation than north slopes. Lakes and ponds or clearings also can provide clues if they are ringed by deciduous trees. The trees on the north side of the opening receive more sunshine, leaf out first, and consequently drop their leaves earlier than trees on the other three sides. Closely observe the green plants. Some indicate directions. The compass goldenrod (*Solidage nemoralis*) puts forth a brilliant flower that usually points north. The rosinweed (*Silphium laciniatum*) flowering head faces east and does not follow the sun. Prairie dock (*Silphium terebinthinaceum*) and prickly lettuce (*Lactuca scariola*) both have leaves that point north and south.

All these methods of finding

Figure 5–4

Shadow sticks used for finding directions. Using the longer stick's shadow, the shorter sticks lie east and west of each other when placed in the ground ½ hour apart.

Figure 5–5

Sight across two sticks at a star. If it rises, you are looking east. If it moves to the left, you are looking north. If it falls, you're looking west. If it moves right, you're looking south.

the directions should be practiced and committed to memory before an emergency develops. Then they will be second nature.

A Scenario

Let's set up a scenario that could easily occur to hunters, anglers, photographers, or sight-seers who contract a light plane to fly them over remote territory. The plane is forced to crash land and the pilot is killed. Your are on your own. After a few hours the shock of the accident will wear off, and you will start to think about getting out on your own. A flight plan was not filed, therefore a search party might not be initiated for several days. Thinking back over the journey, you remember seeing a highway out the right window. The sun was shining into the airplane from the left-hand side. The time was about noon.

At noon the sun is in the southern sky, therefore the highway must lie to the north since it was visible in the opposite direction. Now you know you will have to walk in a northern direction to get out, but cloudy weather has set in, and you don't have a compass. You think you know which direction is north, but you're not sure. You wisely decide to wait until the sky clears so you can tell directions. Finally about an hour after dark, the clouds roll back and the stars are visible. In the brief time that the sky is clear, you spot the Little Dipper, and realize that if you walk toward the Little Dipper, you will be walking toward the highway. You prudently decide to wait until daylight to start walking, and so you don't forget which direction you were looking when you spotted the Little Dipper, you create a marker pointing toward it. This marker can be a long stick, a line of stones, or even an arrow drawn in the dirt or snow. Next morning you set out, and by aligning trees and other natural objects, you continue to walk in a straight line. In six hours you stumble onto the highway and help soon arrives.

Part II

The Global Positioning System

Learning the Basics

P unch in a few numbers and head into the woods or across the lake to that secret fishing hot spot. Then punch in a few more numbers and return to where you started. It sounds easy, convenient, and foolproof, but as with many surefire "solutions," getting the most from your GPS receiver is not as easy as it seems at first blush. In fact, countless enthusiastically purchased receivers now sit unused, collecting dust, beause their owners couldn't figure out how to use them effectively. This section is for the thousands of outdoor enthusiasts who own a GPS receiver and can't use it. It's also for those of you who want to buy a receiver but don't know which one and have no idea how to start the shopping process. It's a basic introduction to the concepts and capabilities of GPS. It aims to get you started by helping you understand how GPS works and how to make it work for you, providing a short list of available receivers and their features, and offering some guidance on what you should look for when you shop for a GPS unit. Later sections direct you to where you can learn more and get some hands-on instruction that can help you take full advantage of your unit with only a small time investment.

Anyone can learn to operate a GPS receiver.

Actually, It *Is* Rocket Science

lthough you don't need a Ph.D. to use GPS, the system was designed by some pretty high-level scientists, and it's awfully complex. Knowing something about the system can help you understand and unravel challenges you encounter in the field. Let me start by giving you a cursory overview of how GPS came about and how it works.

Developed by the U.S. Department of Defense (DoD) in the 1970s, the Global Positioning System, or GPS, consists of a constellation of twenty-four satellites orbiting the earth every twelve hours at an altitude of around 11,000 miles. These satellites continuously transmit signals that can be picked up by receivers located anywhere on earth to provide incredibly accurate information about position, velocity, and time. By using coordinates—two numbers that refer to the exact spot where a horizontal line (latitude, for example) and a vertical line (such as longitude) intersect, a GPS receiver can precisely determine its location, anywhere, at any time, in any weather, day or night. Stop and think about that one. It's a quantum leap forward in navigation and positioning technology.

Once the device determines where it is, it can continuously or periodically update that position to tell you which way you're heading and how fast you're traveling. Although the system was developed for the U.S. military, anyone in the world who cares to purchase a GPS receiver can obtain and use these signals completely free of charge.

The former Soviet Union developed a similar system, known as GLONASS (*GLO*bal *NA*vigation Satellite System). Although this system's constellation has been in decline since the breakup of the USSR, some GLONASS satellites are still operational. Because it uses slightly different technology, GLONASS signals are only compatible with a few specially designed GPS/GLONASS receivers, most of which are very expensive and

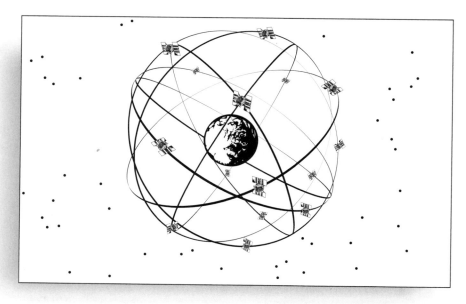

Figure 6-1

The Global Positioning System consists of twenty-four satellites orbiting the earth.

intended for highly specialized markets. For future reference, though, it's good to know GLONASS is out there (or, rather, up there) because the European Community is considering renovating the system and providing its signals as a competitor to GPS.

While the original mission of GPS was to help U.S. military personnel pinpoint the positions of soldiers, weapons, and targets, once the civilian population got wind of the benefits of this emerging technology during the 1990s, the market evolved at an amazing pace. Companies began making receivers faster, better, and cheaper, and marketing them to mainstream consumers. The results of this commercial proliferation were astounding. The first military receivers in the 1980s, for example, cost around $65,000 and weighed nearly sixty-five pounds each. During Operation Desert Storm in the early 1990s—the first large-scale deployment of handheld GPS receivers—U.S. troops relied on units weighing about 3.5 pounds to maneuver soldiers, helicopters, and tanks behind enemy lines. Today many handheld units weigh less than a pound, easily slip into a hip pocket, and sell for as little as $99.

As prices plummeted and the number of GPS receivers on the market soared, ever more inventive ways of using the technology emerged.

Figure 6–2

Signals bounce off the satellites, then back down to your handheld receiver.

Today GPS receivers are being installed on golf carts to help players determine the distance between holes. Integrated GPS and cellular communication systems are now offered as a standard feature in many high-end automobiles, enabling motorists to navigate city streets; contact emergency personnel and instantly provide the dispatcher with the vehicle's precise location; and access concierge services to determine, for example, which hotel or restaurant of choice is closest to the vehicle's current position. Climbers have taken GPS receivers to the top of Everest, explorers have used them to map the location of ancient ruins, and some of the hardiest athletes in the world have used them to navigate the grueling Iditarod dogsled race, even in whiteout conditions. Among the most popular and fastest-growing recreational uses for GPS receivers in the United States today, though, are boating and backcountry navigation for hikers, hunters, anglers, snowmobilers, cross-country skiers, and anyone else who likes to put themselves in the middle of nowhere, and then come back again.

GPS receivers can also help out when tragedy strikes. When Alaska Airlines Flight 261 went down off the California coast on January 31, 2000, the National Oceanic and Atmospheric Administration used GPS

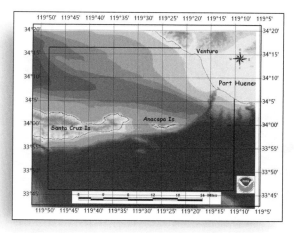

Figure 6-3
....

GPS receivers have proven invaluable in emergency situations. When Alaska Flight 261 went down off the California coast, rescuers used GPS to organize search and salvage efforts.

receivers to establish search grids for the U.S. Navy and U.S. Coast Guard search vessels to follow. When debris was located and later recovered, its exact location was recorded using GPS coordinates. Recovery vessels were able to locate relatively small portions of the downed aircraft by heading to the precise coordinate. The rescue and salvage personnel created maps using the GPS coordinates that would later be used to analyze the crash site during the investigation.

A group of climbers took GPS receivers to the top of Kilimanjaro in Africa recently to measure the mountain's height. GPS coordinates were so precise, even with the intentional inaccuracies programmed into the signals by Selective Availability for national security purposes, they were able to determine that the mountain's height was 5,892 meters—three meters lower than previously thought.

Talking GPS

This section will focus on just a few of the most elemental navigation tools that a GPS receiver can provide: your position in terms of coordinates, the direction to a specified waypoint, the distance to that waypoint, and your speed and direction of travel. Some of these terms may be new to many of you. So before we take the discussion any farther, let's define a few of the terms and concepts you're going to encounter as you delve into GPS.

A *position fix* is your location on earth as determined by the GPS receiver. This position fix can be displayed as a pair of coordinates, such as latitude/longitude (lat/long) or Universal Transverse Mercator (UTM). The position fix as determined by your GPS receiver is usually within about 100 meters or so of your actual location on the earth. In other words, it ain't perfect, and you'll learn why later. Once you obtain a position fix, you can assign it a name and store it in your GPS receiver's memory. This is known as a *waypoint.*

Waypoints can be created in several ways to accomplish different goals. For example, if you want the receiver to document the location of your camp, you can stand at the campsite, obtain a position fix, and name it "camp," thus creating a waypoint that can later help you navigate back to your campsite. Or you might use a map to determine a set of coordinates you wish to reach, then store it as a waypoint to help you navigate to this destination. Or to ensure that you can retrace your path at day's end, you could enter waypoints at significant turning points along a path, leaving a virtual breadcrumb trail to follow on your return trip.

You can then use the GPS receiver to determine the distance and direction between any two waypoints or along a

Figure 6-4

By punching in waypoints, you can generate an electronic "map" of your route, then simply retrace your steps to get home.

series of waypoints. And once you start traveling, you can reference the receiver to see your approximate speed of travel, ensure that you're still headed in the right direction, figure out where you are on the map at any given time during the journey, and estimate your travel time and arrival time based on these factors.

If you think you could benefit from these functions, then perhaps you're ready to invest some time and a little gray matter to learn about how GPS determines its location. Here comes the technical part. It doesn't read like a Clancy novel, but having this background knowledge could help you troubleshoot any problems you encounter when you first begin to use your receiver in the field. Don't panic; what follows will be as brief and to the point as possible.

Dissecting the System

GPS is made up of three segments. The *user segment* is composed of the receivers in the hands of individuals on the ground—people like you, me, Mike, and Jim. The *control segment* is a network of DoD-operated ground stations that provide control information to each of the satellites in the constellation. And finally, the *space segment* consists of the twenty-four satellites in orbit around the earth, plus a few spares.

To determine its position, a GPS receiver must obtain *satellite lock* (also referred to as a *fix* or *acquisition*) on at least three GPS satellites. To lock onto a satellite signal, a GPS receiver must have a clear view of the sky. Steep canyons, excessive tree canopy, and proximity to tall trees or buildings can limit this visibility, impeding the satellite lock. Once the signal is acquired, the receiver automatically obtains satellite constellation data (referred to as *almanac* data), which is continuously transmitted by each satellite. Almanac data includes information about the location and health, or operational status, of each satellite. With the signal

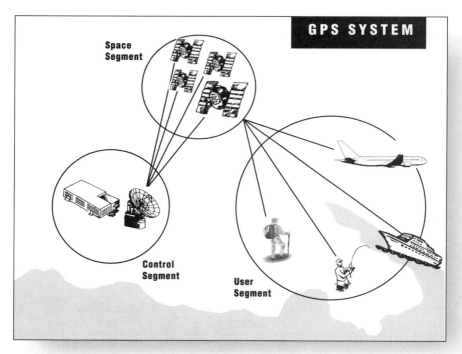

Figure 6-5

There are three links in the GPS chain—the space segment, the control segment, and the user segment.

and almanac data, the receiver instantly begins to calculate its position.

Each satellite's radio signal is stamped with the time when it is sent. When the receiver acquires the first fix, it measures how long it took for the satellite signal to arrive. Using this measurement, the receiver calculates its distance from the satellite. With the signal from the second satellite, the receiver narrows its location on the ground to the two points where the arcs intersect, as illustrated in figure 6-6. When the receiver locks onto the third satellite signal, it uses a technique called *triangulation* to determine its location. The more satellites it can lock onto, the more accurate a position fix the receiver can provide—to a point, that is, because the DoD intentionally degrades the precision level that a civilian GPS receiver can achieve as a matter of national security.

As you recall, GPS signals were originally intended to be used as a U.S. military tool, but are now available to anyone in the world free of charge. In the past, to prevent potentially hostile nations from obtaining the most accurate signals—centimeter level or better, which could be used to very accurately target a missile, for example—DoD used a technique known as *Selective Availability,* or *SA,* to degrade the signal. Receivers in the hands of U.S. military personnel were, of course, not affected by SA. Civilian GPS receivers, however, could generally obtain a reading accurate to anywhere from 30 to 100 meters. In 1996 President Clinton signed a Presidential Decision Directive vowing to turn SA off

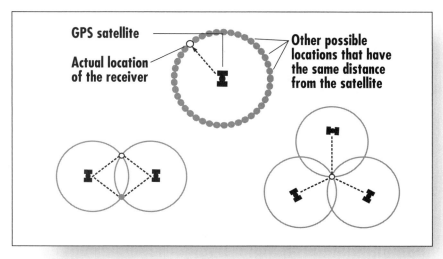

Figure 6-6

GPS receivers establish your position by triangulating coordinates received from at least three satellites.

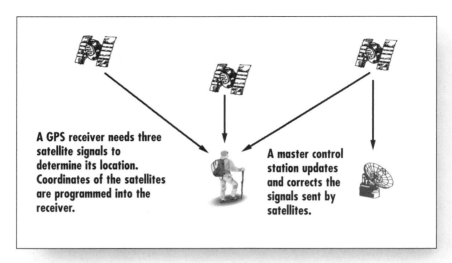

Figure 6-7
....

Data received by triangulating satellite coordinates, combined with signal updates from ground control stations, provide an accurate fix.

within four to ten years. And on May 1, 2000, this finally happened. Civilians can now achieve the same centimeter-level accuracy as personnel in the military. A reading accurate to 10 meters is now possible. At any time, however, the government can turn SA back on. (This would occur, for example, in a time of war.)

Prior to SA being disabled, various techniques were devised by GPS manufacturers to significantly improve this accuracy, and a technique known as *differential GPS,* or *DGPS,* could bring that figure down to the centimeter level by broadcasting correction signals from ground-based beacons. As you would expect, though, DGPS receivers were much more expensive and were generally only purchased by those who required great precision, such as surveyors and engineers.

So in a nutshell, that's what GPS is and how it works. Now that you know how it works, let me discuss how it can help you.

Using and Troubleshooting Your GPS

GPS receiver can be used by itself—as a backup in case you get lost or to help you find an otherwise unmarked location at a future time—or it can be used in conjunction with a map. GPS by itself would be the perfect way to record the location of a hot fishing spot next time you pull in a big one, then return to it later to try your luck again. If you were using GPS with a map, it would provide you with the perfect way to find a remote mountain lake with legendary trout by finding the coordinates on a map and using GPS to navigate to them.

Before we discuss how to accomplish either of these tasks, let's talk about the fundamentals of GPS operation. Remember, when you're using a GPS receiver, you're already subject to errors of 10 or more meters depending on the kind of GPS receiver used. And having a position fix of less than 100 meters most of the time is sufficient for locating trail junctions, campsites, and geographic features. Still, inaccuracies can often be introduced through operator errors, so let's investigate some typical user errors and techniques to help avoid them.

It's Not a Compass!

First, you don't want to use your receiver as a compass. A GPS receiver cannot tell you which direction it's pointing; it can only tell you which direction it's moving. Even then, it's not accurate at walking speeds of less than 10 miles per hour. Also, using your GPS receiver as a compass means consuming precious batteries. Considering the weight burden of carrying a lot of spares, it's probably better to conserve than to replace. Consequently, it's most effective to use your GPS receiver in conjunction with a magnetic compass. Turn on the receiver to get a fix and obtain the bearing to your next destination, then shut it down and use the compass to stay on course.

Look Up!

Second, because the receiver relies on acquiring data from satellites orbiting overhead, the receiver's antenna must have a clear view of the sky to provide accurate information. It takes at least four satellites for a GPS receiver to provide a three-dimensional position fix, which gives horizontal coordinates plus elevation. Although a receiver can provide a two-dimensional fix when only three satellites are being tracked, this offers merely horizontal coordinates and can result in huge errors, sometimes as much as several miles. Obviously, you don't want to operate in 2D mode.

To lock onto as many satellites as possible, make sure you are clear of overhead obstructions before attempting to get a position fix. Look around. Is there a thick tree canopy overhead? If the leaves are wet, the receiver will be fighting what's known as *multipath interference* (the radio signal bounces off other objects before being received by your GPS unit). With multipath in play your receiver may have a hard time obtaining a constant signal even if the canopy isn't thick. Are you near a cliff wall? Are you next to a tall building? Are you within city limits? Urban canyons created by tall buildings can also obstruct signals. Make sure that you are standing somewhere with a clear view of the sky.

Patience Is a Virtue

Third, you must have good *satellite geometry* (referring to the position of the satellites in the sky) to achieve the most accurate position fix possible. Although local obstructions, such as a tree canopy or cliffs, are the most likely causes of poor satellite geometry, it can also occur when satellites are clustered immediately overhead or aligned in a straight line. If your receiver fails to achieve a satellite lock within a few minutes, satellite geometry may be the cause. The receiver tells you how good or how poor its geometry is by providing a measurement known as *dilution of precision (DOP)* or *position dilution of precision (PDOP)*. Generally, the larger the number, the worse your geometry and the poorer your accuracy.

Because the orbiting satellites are constantly changing position, though, geometry often improves if you just give it some time. And oddly enough, if you can't get good geometry, you can sometimes help the receiver "clear its head" by shutting it off for a few moments, then turning it back on (kind of like banging on the side of your TV when the horizontal hold goes haywire!). Consult your receiver's manual for that particular unit's acceptable DOP levels and other troubleshooting tips specific to your GPS device.

A Receiver on Its Own

Every point in the world has an address. Whether it's expressed in latitude/longitude, Universal Transverse Mercator (UTM), or townships and ranges, a set of coordinates exists to refer to every point on earth. The benefit of using a GPS receiver is that you can record this address, no matter how remote it is, and use it for navigation.

When you're using a GPS receiver by itself, you can store these addresses as waypoints in the unit's memory. When you travel away from those waypoints, you can obtain the distance and direction back to them. Once you've learned how to operate your unit, this is a pretty simple process—somewhat like leaving a trail of bread crumbs to follow back to your starting point.

To begin, turn on your receiver. Yes, this should go without saying. Still, if you've traveled a long way since the last time you turned on your receiver, it could take as long as ten or fifteen minutes for the unit to figure out where it is. You can either plug it into your vehicle's cigarette lighter to conserve batteries (assuming you have an adapter) and set it on the hood to process while you pack your bags and fill your water bottles—or you can give it some help using a process called *initialization*. You initialize your receiver by entering the approximate coordinates (telling it where it is). This helps speed the satellite acquisition process.

If you plan to refer to a map at all during your hike, you'll want to tell the receiver what type of coordinate system you'll be using, generally latitude/longitude or UTM. Your receiver probably offers other options as well, which you can set for your convenience. These may include speed units (miles per hour versus kilometers per hour), distance units (metric, nautical miles), and language preference.

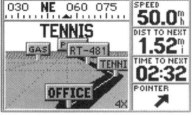

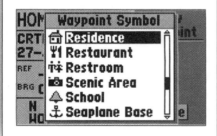

Figure 8-1

GPS receivers provide graphic screens and menu choices for plotting waypoints.

Now that the receiver has initialized, you're tracking at least four satellites, you've achieved a 3D position, and you've selected the language of choice, proceed to the trailhead. Stop and obtain a position fix and save this as your starting waypoint. Of course, you'll learn the proper procedure for doing this from your receiver's instruction manual, but it's generally as easy as pressing a MARK button.

Next, name the position. Again, this is generally very simple and is done using an icon or a pull-down menu (depending on the receiver) and a simple naming convention. You may want to keep a position log by jotting down the name of the waypoint, its coordinates, and the direction of travel when you depart the waypoint (based on a magnetic compass bearing) for an added margin of safety. Once you've noted the location of your departure point, shut off the receiver to save batteries and proceed on your way.

After every thirty or so minutes of hiking, or at each trail juncture, stop, get a position fix, name the waypoint, and jot it down. To avoid confusion, it's simplest to use a sequential numeric naming convention, calling the trailhead "start," then every turn after that follows in sequence as "turn1," "turn2," and so forth.

Once you've completed your hike and are ready to return, simply select the last waypoint (generally using a pull-down menu) that you saved and tell your receiver to "go to" that location. With many receivers, you simply press the button labeled GO TO. The receiver will then provide you with an arrow indicating which direction you must travel, as well as the compass bearing to follow. It will also indicate distance to the next waypoint.

Remember, it's best to get the bearing, then shut off the receiver to conserve batteries, relying on your compass to navigate to the waypoint. When you reach each waypoint, choose the next waypoint and enter GO TO (or the equivalent function button on your unit) to repeat the process. If you've saved in numeric sequence, you simply proceed backward through the course until you've reached the trailhead.

This is the perfect way to ensure, for example, that you can relocate your favorite fishing holes. The next time you catch some award-winning salmon, you can simply initialize your receiver, get a position fix, and hit MARK to record the spot as a waypoint. You'll probably have to call the waypoint "whopper" or something. Then the next time you put your boat in the water, you just select GOTO/WHOPPER and follow a magnetic compass bearing or the GPS receiver's direction arrow (remember, you're speeding along in a boat, so the compass directions become more reliable) back to the hot spot.

GPS receivers are easy to use, and they become easier with each new product generation. Still, they are not a replacement for solid map and compass skills. Next, we'll discuss using your GPS receiver with a map.

GPS and a Map– The Best of Both Worlds

This chapter will discuss how to use GPS, a compass, and a map to create a route of addresses you wish to reach, then follow the receiver's directions to get there. Although much of this discussion assumes you are familiar with map reading and compass use, let's briefly review the basics of map reading using a USGS topo map as an example.

USGS Topo Maps

As we discussed in Part I, among the most commonly used maps for backcountry navigation are USGS (U.S. Geological Survey) 7.5-minute topographic maps, also known as *quadrangles*, or *quad maps*. Each of these large-scale maps covers about 55 square miles and measures around 22 by 27 inches. The USGS has produced about fifty-four thousand 7.5-minute maps to completely cover the United States. I'll use the examples in figures 9-1 through 9-4 to help you become familiar with the basic elements on the map.

Along the Bottom Margin

On the left side of the bottom margin is information about who created, edited, and published the map, along with the date of initial publication and the last time the map was field-checked (figure 9-1). This date clearly points out one of the drawbacks of topo maps. Many of them were created in the 1950s or 1960s and haven't been field-checked for decades. Although some have been edited and revised more recently

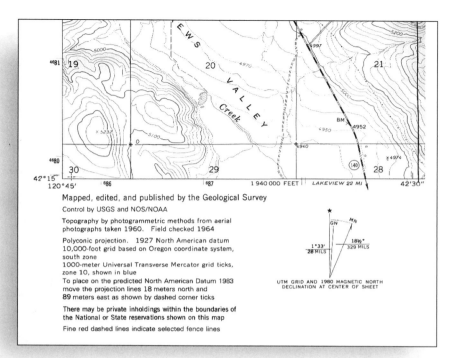

Figure 9-1
....

The left side of a U.S. Geological Survey map includes information about who created the map, the date of initial publication, the datum, and the magnetic declination.

using aerial photos and other source data, much of the more recent source data has not been field-checked. Consequently, many newer trails may not appear on the map, and some trails and roads that no longer exist are still shown. As an example of how disastrous this could be, imagine trying to navigate Mount St. Helens with a topo map that hadn't been field-checked since 1979. To remedy this situation, you can generally contact a local U.S. Forest Service or Department of Natural Resources office for updated information. Despite the dates, though, topos are still among the best low-distortion maps available. As with anything else in backcountry navigation, common sense will make up for their deficiencies.

Right below the edit and field-check dates, you'll find a reference to the datum on which the map is based. The *datum* is the spatial foundation of the map, or what ties it to the real world. You'll want to ensure that the horizontal datum setting in your GPS receiver matches the datum of the map. USGS maps generally use North American Datum 1927 or 1983 (NAD27 or NAD83) or World Geodetic System 1984 (WGS84). Setting your receiver's datum is easily done through one of its menu functions (see the instructions for your specific unit). This allows the receiver to align its readouts to the same spatial reference system used by the mapmakers.

Other notes in this bottom left-hand corner include references about coordinate systems, including Universal Transverse Mercator (UTM) grid ticks (which generally appear in blue) and which UTM zone this map falls into. The Cougar Peak topo map that we're using as an example falls into Zone 10.

The UTM grid system specifies coordinates within a rectangular framework, making it possible to directly link the coordinate numbering system to a distance-measuring system. Whew! Simply put, UTM numbers are easier to work with because they're expressed in units of meters, rather than hours and minutes and seconds (as latitude and longitude are). Because most people are more familiar with latitude/longitude, I'll use that coordinate system in my references. Still, UTM is the wave of the future, and learning it is certainly worth your time—but that's another book!

Immediately to the right of this information is a diagram reflecting magnetic declination; use this when adjusting your compass. Keep in mind that declination changes over time, so you may want to double-check with the U.S. Forest Service or Department of Natural Resources to ensure that you are using the correct adjusted figure.

The map's scale can be found at the center of the bottom margin (figure 9-2). Generally drawn at a 1:24,000 scale (except for Alaska, which is at 1:63,360), each inch on a USGS topo map equals about 2,000 feet on the ground.

Immediately below the map scale is a reference to the map's contour intervals, which are generally 20 feet on USGS maps. Contours appear as brown lines on topographic maps, with all points along the same line being at approximately the same elevation. In other words, if you follow a contour interval on the ground, you're walking along level ground. If you're crossing over contour intervals, you're either climbing or descending. Using these lines, you can easily estimate slope based on the distance between the contour lines: Closer contour lines reflect a steeper grade, and more widely spaced lines indicate a more gradual slope.

Also found along the bottom are the map's location reference—which reflects approximately where the unit falls within the state—and a road legend (figure 9-3).

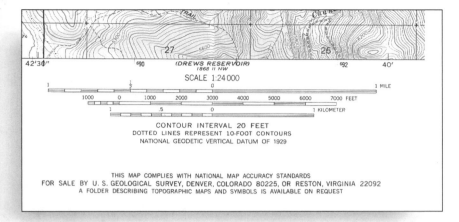

Figure 9-2

At the center of the bottom margin is the scale and a reference to the map's contour intervals.

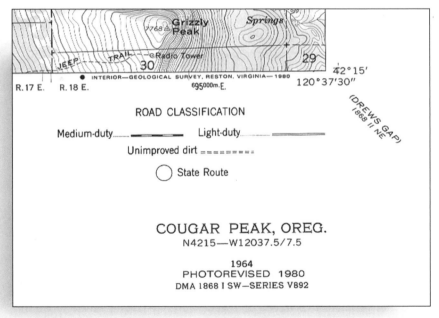

Figure 9-3

The bottom right corner includes the map's location reference and a road legend.

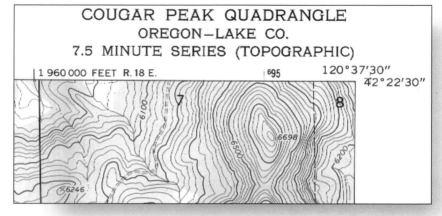

COUGAR PEAK QUADRANGLE
OREGON–LAKE CO.
7.5 MINUTE SERIES (TOPOGRAPHIC)

Figure 9-4

The name of a USGS map appears in its top right-hand corner.

Everywhere Else

The name of the map appears in its top right-hand corner (figure 9-4). In parentheses in each corner of the map, you will find the name of the adjacent quadrangle. If you know that you'll be traveling off the map you're using, this reference tells you the name of the next map you'll need to continue your journey.

Along the outside lines of the map (known as the *neatlines*) are the UTM tick lines (in blue), latitude and longitude tick marks (in black) at 2.5-minute intervals on a quad, road destinations, and townships and ranges (in red).

Paper or Plastic?

Paper topo maps are readily available at outdoor recreation stores, from surveyor's outlets, and through a variety of federal agencies, such as the U.S. Forest Service, the USGS, and the Bureau of Land Management. They are also available electronically. These digital topo maps, known as *DRGs* or *digital raster graphics*, are high-resolution scanned versions of the paper originals that have been "geo-referenced." This enables you to point your cursor at a desired location on the map and click to determine its coordinates, which you can then use to program a route into your GPS receiver. These digital products can even interface with your GPS receiver through a serial port to download coordinates. Again, check with your local outdoor retailer for availability. For now let's stick to discussing how to use your GPS receiver in conjunction with a paper map.

Map and GPS Together

If you're familiar with maps, you can use them to plan a route and input that route into your GPS receiver. I'll walk through an example using my Cougar Peak quadrangle and latitude/longitude. As we discussed in chapter 8, you'll still want to store the trailhead and other significant locations as waypoints in your receiver (as a backup route) so that you can retrace your steps if necessary.

Planning a Route

To create a route in your GPS receiver, first look at your map and determine where your hike will begin, where you want to go, and which route you wish to follow. Where is the trailhead and where will you turn around? Once you've made these decisions, you'll want to consider the intermediate waypoints—all the in-between places where you'll want to gauge your progress or need significant direction changes, such as at trail junctions, creeks, valleys, streams, and other distinct features. Use the contour lines (they help you see where slopes are steep and where they are gradual) to determine where gulleys are to be avoided, where to find notches or passes that might make your route a bit easier, or what geographic features might make it more interesting.

Once you've drawn your route on the map, use a latitude/ longitude ruler or UTM reader to determine the coordinates of each major milestone along the way. Make a list of these coordinates on a journal that you can take with you (laminated or sealed in a plastic baggie, of course) as a backup.

Now load the route into your receiver's memory. To do this:

1. Make sure that you have entered the correct datum (from the map's lower left-hand corner) into your receiver.

2. Using the list you made (and referring to your map), enter the coordinates of each waypoint into your receiver's memory.

3. Name each waypoint using a feature name or sequential numeric designation. Jot the names of these waypoints next to the coordinates in your field journal.

If your planned route has more waypoints than will fit into one of your receiver's routes, break the trip into multiple routes and overlap the ending waypoints. If your receiver has a route-reversal feature, you won't need to create a route for the return portion of an out-and-back trip; simply reverse the route.

Remember, you're already dealing with the errors introduced by Selective Availability, so try to be as accurate as possible when you input coordinates from a map. If you're not familiar with how to read coordinates from a map, there are a lot of good books on the subject, and many community colleges and outdoor stores offer short courses on it as well.

With your route planned and plugged into your receiver, you can use your GPS unit to get to the trailhead. If the trailhead is remote, you can use the same route-finding process to get there. Simply look at the map and determine the coordinates of each road junction along the way. Enter each junction along the drive into your GPS receiver as a waypoint. Then plug your receiver (assuming again that you have the cigarette-lighter power-cord adapter) into your cigarette lighter, make sure you're operating in the right datum and tracking enough satellites to get a three-dimensional fix, then use your receiver's GOTO function to get directions to each successive waypoint. While traveling in a car, the receiver's direction arrow is more reliable than when you're on foot. Remember, though, that because the road twists and turns, the receiver will often indicate you're traveling in the wrong direction. Routes over land rarely travel as the crow flies. But if you've entered the data right, you should still be on course.

If you have difficulty getting a good signal with the receiver inside the car, try moving it around. A friend of mine once traveled through Arizona using his GPS receiver in a Mazda 626. When the unit was placed on the dash, it couldn't get good reception, but when he set it in the console between the seats (where the antenna could track through both the extremely sloped front and back windshields), it instantly acquired a position fix and held it reliably. So get creative and move the unit around, keeping in mind the goal of the best possible view of the sky. Or if you have a remote antenna, try placing that in the best possible location to get a good sky view.

At the Trailhead

Once you've reached the trailhead, ensure that your position fix compares closely with the stored trailhead waypoint. Even with SA, these numbers should be within a few seconds of latitude/longitude. If they're off by more than that, double-check your calculations before heading into the back woods relying on your planned coordinates. Are you operating in three-dimensional mode? If you're not acquiring enough satellites to get a reliable fix, what's the problem? Are you next to a sheer cliff wall? Is there a tree canopy overhead that's blocking your signal? Is the receiver using the correct datum?

Once you've verified the accuracy of your trailhead position, you should be able to proceed with confidence. Use the GOTO function of your receiver to determine the bearing and distance to each successive waypoint. After obtaining distance and direction, turn off the receiver to conserve batteries, and use your compass to verify direction along the way. Remember, a GPS receiver is not a good indicator of compass bearing anyway, because it only provides direction of travel when you're on the move at more than 10 miles per hour. Periodically turn on the receiver to ensure that you're still on the right track, then shut it down again. At each waypoint turn on the receiver again to ensure that your stored waypoint matches the current position fix to within a couple of hundred yards or a few seconds of latitude/longitude. If they don't match up, store these new position fixes as waypoints and use them to navigate back if necessary.

On the Receiving End

A lthough dozens of GPS receivers are available with wide-ranging "bells and whistles" as well as wide price ranges, every model can accomplish the basic tasks we've discussed. The device can tell you approximately where you are (coordinates), the direction (or bearing) you are traveling when you're moving at a speed greater than 10 miles per hour, the distance to your destination (or waypoint), the speed (velocity) at which you are traveling, when you will reach your destination if you continue to travel at the same rate of speed (estimated time of arrival), and how long the total journey will take (time en route) if these factors remain the same. The trick, then, is to give some thought to your own specific needs before you select a receiver.

Which Receiver Is Right for You?

Okay, it's not a life-altering decision like getting married or quitting your nine-to-five job to become a rafting guide, but you should still carefully consider which features are most important to you before you head to a sporting goods store.

If you plan to use your receiver for multiday backcountry hiking, for example, weight is at a premium, so you may want to choose the lightest receiver possible. You may also want to consider how long the unit will operate on a set of batteries. Remember, spare batteries mean extra weight in your pack that could otherwise have been allocated to a couple of extra energy bars!

For winter sports you'll need a receiver with the lowest minimum operating temperature possible. You should also select a unit that works with lithium or ni-cad batteries, which perform better than alkalines in cold weather.

If you're a hunter you'll probably require the most rugged receiver available, and one with an internal antenna—which is less likely to be bent or broken off as you sling that record whitetail over your shoulder to return to camp. You'll also want to ensure that your receiver is water resistant for those damp fall mornings and stream crossings, as well as for slogging after waterfowl.

Anglers and paddlers may want to choose a completely waterproof unit that can actually float and survive being fully submerged.

If you plan to use the unit to navigate the roads to a trailhead, you'll want to use your vehicle's battery to power the unit. Consequently, you'll need a cigarette-lighter adapter. You'll also want a receiver capable of accommodating an extended or remote antenna. This enables you to place the unit on a seat or console and extend the antenna to the vehicle's dash or windshield, providing a better view of the sky and, consequently, more reliable reception.

After considering your basic needs, you can shop for the bells and whistles you want and decide whether you're willing to pay for them. These can include built-in maps, audible alarms, and course deviation indicators. For land navigation the more useful features include automatic route reversal, a battery-strength indicator, and a sunlight-readable display.

Keep these functions and your needs in mind as we take a quick look at the receivers currently available on the market and their approximate prices. Remember, though, that this is a rapidly growing market; many new units will have been introduced by the time this book gets to print. Each GPS receiver manufacturer tends to come out with a couple of new models or upgrades to existing units each year, so you'll probably have an even wider selection than that presented. And who knows— maybe the price has already dropped on some of these units. Also, keep in mind that we're not endorsing or providing performance reviews of these units. We're simply providing you with information about what is available, as well as some background information about the top three manufacturers of consumer-oriented GPS products.

The Big Three

The GPS market is basically divided into two sectors: professional and consumer. The professional market includes surveyors, engineers, and others who need extremely precise measurements. Trimble, Leica, NavAtel, Ashtech, and Javad Positioning Systems are some of the larger manufacturers of professional GPS receivers. What's more important to you are the big three in consumer GPS receivers.

Two of the largest GPS manufacturers in the world, Magellan and Lowrance, merged in 1999 to create a $150-million satellite-based consumer and recreational business under the Magellan banner.

Magellan offered the first handheld GPS receiver in 1989, and has sold

Figure 10-1
....

The decision of which GPS receiver is right for you depends on your needs for durability, functionality, weight, and battery life.

more than two million GPS devices since that time. Today the company specializes in satellite-access products, including mapping products for marine uses, outdoor recreation, vehicle navigation, and general aviation; handheld GPS receivers; satellite telephones; and two-way satellite messaging units. It's one of the few companies that markets a combined GPS/GLONASS receiver, which I discussed in chapter 6.

Lowrance electronics has been a leading player in the marine and recreational electronics business for more than forty years. The company introduced the world's first commercial sonar instrument for sport fishing in 1957. Since then Lowrance has sold more than five million sonar units. It introduced its first GPS product for the boating and fishing markets in 1991 and later expanded its product offerings into the hunting, hiking, and general aviation markets. The company markets its GPS receivers under both the Lowrance and Eagle brand names.

Founded in 1989, *Garmin International* designs, manufactures, and markets navigation and communications electronics worldwide for consumer, business, and military use, with more than fifty products in its line. The name *Garmin*, by the way, is a combination of the first names of the company's president (Gary Burrell) and its vice president of engineering (Min H. Kao).

Now let's look at some of the products these companies offer, starting with those for automotive navigation. These units will get you to the trailhead—but you won't want to unload them and take them into the woods! Although they are not aimed at the outdoor recreation market, they are interesting enough to talk about.

On the Road

Magellan has introduced a driver information system called the 750NAV. This device uses an extensive digital street map, an immense points-of-interest (landmarks, monuments, and so forth) library, and an embedded Magellan GPS receiver to provide you with turn-by-turn directions. The 750 uses the GPS functions to display a vehicle's real-time location on a small color monitor situated in the vehicle. You enter your destination; the unit will calculate the most direct route, then provide turn-by-turn instructions by synthesized voice command (your choice, male or female!) or by displaying the map on the monitor. For off-road navigation (places that are off the map), four-wheel-drive enthusiasts can simply input waypoints and use the device just as they would a handheld GPS receiver. The unit installs in a "docking station" and, consequently, can be moved from vehicle to vehicle. Magellan and the Hertz Corporation recently installed fifty thousand of these units in Hertz rental cars under the name NeverLost.

Garmin's vehicle navigation product, StreetPilot GPS, is portable, weighs about a pound, and uses a twelve-channel GPS receiver to determine its position. It includes a built-in base map of the entire United States. To obtain street-level detail, you can purchase one of Garmin's plug-in MetroGuide cartridges for the region of interest, then zoom in for more detail or out for the bigger picture. Using the MetroGuide you can look up street addresses, restaurants, and even ATMs near your location with a touch of a button. You can also mark favorite places on the map and link them together to create a route to your destination. You can store as many as five hundred waypoints and thirty reversible routes. The device uses arrows to indicate which way to turn at selected intersections, and can provide distance to the waypoint from your present location as well as estimated time of arrival. Introduced in 2001, the SteetPilot III system provides clear voice prompted turn-by-turn directions. Garmin's GPS V system is its most versatile, with the ability to view it horizontally, for mounting on a dash or a bike, or vertically for handheld use.

These devices can get you to the trailhead and help you find the

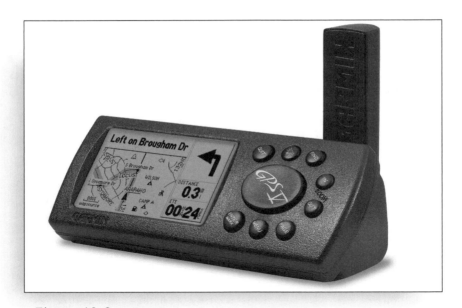

Figure 10-2
....

The Garmin GPS V

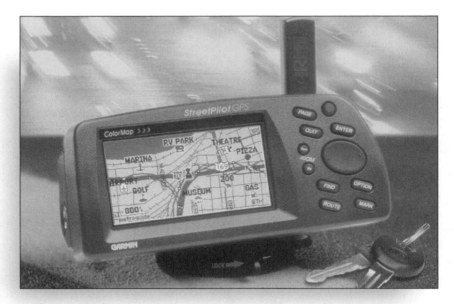

Figure 10-3
....

StreetPilot ColorMap guides you through the urban wilderness.

nearest pizza joint when you're on the way home. Now here are some units you'll actually want to carry into the woods.

On the Trail

For the great outdoors Magellan, Garmin, and Lowrance offer a variety of handheld receivers. I'll give you a quick overview of these twelve-channel receivers, breaking them down into three categories: entry level, a step up, and top of the line. Each of these manufacturers also offers digital maps. If you have a PC, you can often hook up your GPS receiver and download coordinate data from these maps on disk. So I'll also give you an overview of the mapping software available before we're through.

Entry-Level Receivers

Magellan's entry-level units are the pocket-sized GPS 300 and Blazer 12. Each weighs around seven ounces and measures 5 by 2 by 1.3 inches. The 300 can store one hundred waypoints and one route with ten legs, and it operates for twenty-four hours on two AA alkaline batteries. The Blazer 12 can save one hundred waypoints and one reversible and editable route with ten legs; it can operate for twenty hours on two AA alkaline batteries. It shows your speed, the distance and time to your destination, as well as your bearing and heading. Both devices can operate at temperatures as low as 32°F.

It offers 12 parallel channels for fast signal acquistions and stronger lock-ons. It features a built-in custom background map with water, land, and highway detail from southern Canada to northern Mexico, plus Hawaii and Bahamas. Lowrance's GlobalMap 100, available in 2001 for $199, can store 1,750 position points (75 waypoints

Figure 10-4

The Lowrance GlobalMap 100 can store 1,750 position points.

and 1,000 event markers). Lowrance's optional MapCreate custom mapping software let's you high-detail maps. The GlobalMap 100 uses four AA batteries and is completely sealed and waterproof.

Garmin's GPS 12 provides sixteen graphic icons for marking waypoints, and allows you to display these icons with names or comments on the moving map page. The GPS 12 can store five hundred waypoints with twenty reversible routes containing up to thirty waypoints each. The TracBack navigation feature automatically turns your track log into a route back home, without marking waypoints. The GPS 12 features a backlit LCD display, weighs 9.5 ounces, can operate for twelve hours on four AA batteries, and has an internal lithium battery to protect your data. It features waterproof housing, can operate in temperatures as low as 5°F, and sells for around $200.

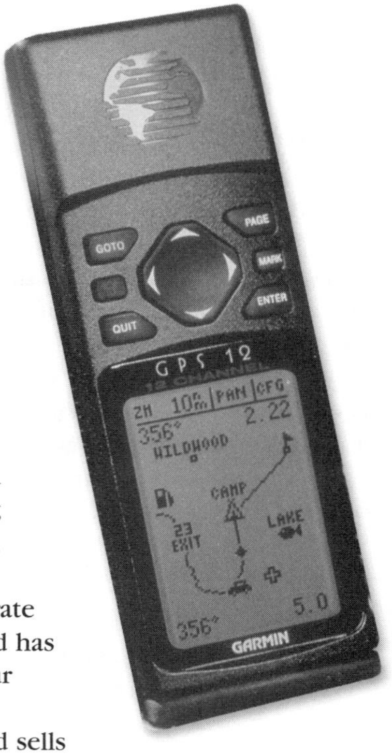

The newest entry to the Garmin line is the extremely compact (and cool-looking) eTrex, which weighs only six ounces and measures only 4 inches high by 2 inches wide. It will literally fit in the palm of your hand. Garmin has placed all the buttons on the sides of this unit, allowing for simple one-handed operation that won't obstruct your view of the display. The eTrex is completely waterproof and will operate for eighteen hours on just two AA batteries. The manufacturers claim that the eTrex will maintain satellite lock under a tree canopy, but I'd test that pretty thoroughly first. It can store five hundred user waypoints with graphic icons, has a route-reversal feature or TracBack function, and sells for around $145.

Figure 10-5

The Garmin eTrex, available in 2002 for less than $150.

A Step Up

For a little more money, you can gain a lot more functionality with Magellan's GPS 315 and GPS 320 receivers. Each of these units weighs less than seven ounces, measures only 6.2 by 2.0 by 1.3 inches, and is built to withstand the elements. With rubber grips and weatherproof construction—they will even float—they can operate for as long as fifteen hours on two AA alkaline batteries and can withstand temperatures as cold as 14°F. You can save as many as five hundred locations of trails, campsites, and hunting and fishing hot spots in either unit's database. Both products incorporate a menu-driven interface that allows you to move from feature to feature to access all the unit's functions. The EZStart initialization feature eliminates the need to input coordinates when you first use the unit. The unit's rocker keypad and dedicated GOTO, MARK, MMNU, and NAV keys make it pretty easy to save and name landmarks and return to them quickly.

The Magellan GPS 315 retails for around $150 and includes a built-in database of nearly twenty thousand cities, which can be used as landmarks in a route or as a destination when using the unit's GOTO function. In addition to five hundred landmarks, the GPS 315 can save twenty routes with as many as thirty legs each. The 315's ten-year lithium battery backup protects this memory when the batteries are removed. Hunters and anglers who like to know the best times to be afield can benefit from the best fish/game calculator, as well as the sunrise/sunset, moonrise/moonset, and lunar-phase data.

The GPS 315 is PC compatible and can access Magellan's DataSend CD-ROM accessory, which sells for under $80. The CD contains thousands of points of interest, including campgrounds, parks, golf courses, and tourist attractions. You can load the CD into your PC, select the desired points of interest for your next trip, then upload them into your GPS receiver for use in navigation. Another benefit of PC compatibility is the ability to transfer locations that you have saved in your GPS receiver back to the PC for storage. This is a pretty convenient way to ensure that you can return to the same hunting hot spot year after year. For those whose adventures occasionally take them offshore or onto marine waterways, DataSend also features a database of worldwide nautical navigation aids, such as buoys, beacons, wrecks, and

Figure 10-6

The Garmin eTrex Venture offers a worldwide database of cities.

Figure 10-7

Lowrance's iFINDER offers virtually unlimited custom mapping capacity.

underwater obstructions.

The GPS 320 is similar to the 315 but enhanced for marine navigation, with a preloaded regional nautical navigation aid database. Three different regional databases are available that cover the Americas, Europe/Africa, and Asia/Australia. The 320 is also PC compatible; it can be uploaded with data from the DataSend accessory. It retails for around $200.

For around $300 Garmin's GPS 12XL is similar to its GPS 12, but has a twenty-four-hour battery life and includes a built-in database of towns and cities, orienteering features like position averaging, and UTM and user grid formats to allow hikers to add their own map parameters. For a bit more money, the GPS 12CX is similar to the 12XL but includes a point database of cities, a battery life of thirty-five hours, and a three-color display screen. It also features dedicated zoom keys for quick map scaling and can store 1,000 waypoints.

Another step up in Garmin's line is eMap, a

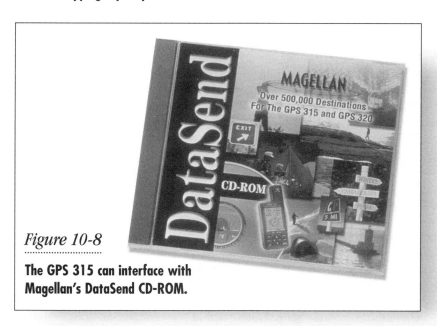

Figure 10-8

The GPS 315 can interface with Magellan's DataSend CD-ROM.

handheld electronic map and GPS receiver with an extra-large display for showing even more map data. The device is designed to go from the car to the hiking trail to the beach. The size of a small calculator, the unit weighs six ounces and can operate for fourteen hours on just two AA batteries. The eMAP features an internal base map comparable to that in the GPS III Plus (see Top-of-the-Line Receivers, below) and is compatible with Garmin MapSource CD-ROMs. It will store sixteen megabytes of downloaded information at a time. It is water resistant, displays with a four-level gray scale, and stores fifty user waypoints. It retails for around $300.

Garmin's eTrex Vista combines all the features of the eTrex (Figure 10-6) with a basemap of North and South America, a barometric altimeter, an electric compass and 24 megabytes of memory. This memory capacity permits the unit to accept downloaded mapping data from CD-ROMs available from the manufacturer, including such things as fishing "Hot Spots." The eTrex Vista features a 12 parallel channel reciever and is, the company notes, its most popular unit with hikers and climbers. It costs around $375.

Figure 10-9

The Garmin eTrex Vista offers an altimeter and an electric compass.

Top-of-the-Line Receivers

At around $650, Lowrance's GlobalMap 12 expands greatly on the built-in mapping of the less expensive Lowrance units. The background map of the entire world boasts increased detail of the forty-eight contiguous states plus the Hawaiian Islands, southern Canada, the Caribbean, and the northern coast of Honduras. The optional Inland Mapping System (IMS) Smart Map mini cartridges—maps on CD-ROM—

includes the names and locations of more than 140,000 cities; thirty thousand national, state, and county parks; and data on waterways, even coastal waters out to 25 miles. These cartridges display this highly detailed information onscreen and show your present position on the map as a blinking cursor. The unit is completely sealed and waterproof.

Lowrance's all-in-one offering for the angler is the LMS-160 Map, a combined high-performance sonar fish finder, GPS receiver, and CD-ROM mapping package. This out-of-the box navigation package features a built-in background map of the world and displays your position as a blinking cursor on the map. The package comes complete with a data transfer cable, AC adapter, upload/download waypoint management software, cigarette-lighter adapter, and IMS CD-ROM.

Figure 10-10

....

The GlobalMap 12 is a 12-channel receiver with enhanced mapping capabilities.

The top of the line in Garmin's handheld units is the twelve-channel GPS III Plus, which sells for around $570. At about nine ounces, this little unit offers cartographic capabilities previously found only in high-end automotive and marine units. Its screen switches between vertical and horizontal orientations, and its enhanced base map of North and South America contains more than ten thousand additional small cities, airport locations, secondary roads within metropolitan areas, rivers, streams, airports, and U.S. state and interstate highways. In addition the GPS III Plus comes with an extensive and detailed database of exit information for the federal interstate highway system, enabling you to find out about food, lodging, service stations, and so forth. By plugging the GPS III Plus into your PC, you can download data from Garmin's optional line of MapSource CD-ROMs, which works with Windows 95, Windows 98, and Windows NT software.

The unit is waterproof and said to be completely submersible. It operates for thirty-six hours on four AA batteries with an internal ten-year lithium battery backup. The package includes a standard PC interface cable, lanyard, and Velcro mount

Figure 10-11

The Garmin GPS III Plus can switch from vertical to horizontal screen display.

for a vehicle dashboard. With this combination of features, the GPS III Plus can be used in the vehicle and then carried as a handheld for backcountry navigation.

For around $350 Magellan offers its Map 410 twelve-channel handheld GPS receiver, which combines a worldwide background map with detailed highway cartography and a database of marine navigational aids. Its built-in base map includes coastlines, cities, lakes, rivers, railroads, interstates, and state highways. Marine navigation aids include floating and fixed buoys, lighthouses, and radio beacons that are displayed as unique icons for easy recognition. The unit is also PC compatible for use with the MapSend CD-ROM. It features a detachable antenna and a much larger display than the 315 or 320.

Hikers can benefit from the unit's built-in altimeter, which provides elevation, and a built-in thermometer for recording the ambient temperature. The unit also includes the sunrise/sunset times, moonrise/moonset times, and a moon-phase calculator for anyplace in the world on any date and time. The Northfinder feature displays sun and moon positions so you can quickly determine your desired direction while standing still. The Map 410 can store five hundred waypoints and

Figure 10-12

The Map 410 is Magellan's 12-channel GPS receiver.

twenty reversible/editable routes with as many as thirty legs.

An automatic position-averaging function reportedly reduces the effects of SA for a more accurate position fix. Because the unit is differential ready, it can be linked to a differential beacon receiver to obtain corrections broadcast by the U.S. Coast Guard or commercial sources to improve its accuracy to around 5 to 10 meters.

Built to withstand the rigors of marine use, the waterproof receiver has wraparound rubber coating, water-sealed battery compartments, and an all-rubber backlit keypad that keeps water and salt spray from penetrating the housing. It's slightly bigger than either the GPS 315 or the GPS 320, measuring 6.3 by 2.5 by 1.4 inches and weighing twelve ounces. The unit uses four AA batteries for thirty hours of operation and includes an internal lithium battery to retain the unit's memory for ten years. An optional power/data/external-antenna kit allows you to operate the unit below deck on a boat or inside a vehicle while the antenna sits outside for better satellite lock.

Electronic Maps

As I mentioned earlier, each of the big three manufacturers also offers maps on CD. And these CD maps make it very easy to download coordinates for route planning if you purchase a PC-compatible receiver.

Garmin's MapSource line of CD-ROMs can be loaded from a PC onto its compatible receivers. For $129 the company's U.S. Topo MapSource provides terrain, contour, and elevation information for use by hikers, skiers, hunters, and other outdoor enthusiasts. It includes digital topographic maps showing highways, roads, trails, elevation contours, streams, rivers, summits, schools, and churches. In addition, with U.S. Topo, mariners can view navigation aids such as daybeacons, radio beacons, lights, buoys, wrecks, and obstructions. The U.S. Roads and

Figure 10-13

MapSource maps provide terrain contour and elevation data for backcountry users.

Recreation CD sells for $99 and provides street-level detail of residential areas plus rivers, streams, lakes, and navigation aids. The Trip and Waypoint Manager with World Map CD sells for around $70 and provides additional streams, rivers, small roads, and islands outside the United States, along with nautical navigational aids worldwide.

IMS MapCreate software from Lowrance is designed to complement the built-in background maps included with most Lowrance products. It includes more than twenty million rural and city street segments along with detailed uploadable database features such as U.S. navigation aids, U.S. coastal wrecks and obstructions, lakes, rivers, and other water bodies for anglers and general boating. Land-based features include U.S. rural roads, railroads, U.S. state roads, and U.S. highways. By choosing any or all of the features (point and click), you can create a customized map of a selected area and upload as much as two megabytes of mapping detail into a compatible Lowrance GPS mapping product.

Figure 10-14

The Yeoman XP1 provides an easy-to-understand interface between GPS and map coordinates.

For those who don't have Windows 95, Garmin offers IMS MapSelect, which contains sixty-four maps with predefined boundaries that include the names and locations of more than 140,000 cities; thirty thousand national, state, and county parks; 120,000 bodies of water; and more. MapSelect also includes a waypoint, route, icon, and trail manager. This data management software allows you to download and save information from your receiver for editing and future trip planning back to the same location.

Magellan's GPS Map N Track software is aimed at street navigation. Using your PC, you can pick any two addresses or points to create a door-to-door route and then print detailed driving instructions. Or you can connect your GPS receiver and download this plan; your receiver will point the way. Magellan's DataSend CD-ROM enables you to customize the GPS 315 or GPS 320 with its database of more than five hundred thousand points of interest in the United States. Select from more than thirty-five categories of locations, including cities, campgrounds, golf courses, and tourist attractions. Then you can upload the POIs into your receiver to have the coordinates at your fingertips at any time.

In addition to the big three, several other mapmakers offer maps on CD-ROM. DeLorme's 3-D TopoQuads, for example, include seamless USGS topographic coverage for the entire United States. With this software you can search by place-name, geographic feature, USGS quad, or latitude and longitude. You can profile your hikes and backcountry travels for distance, elevation, grade, and more, and view a three-dimensional perspective of any area in the United States. Maps can be customized with symbols, text, and notes. You can print maps and even a cross-sectional profile of your planned route. And of course, you can download maps and routes to your GPS receiver, as well as to a palm computer or handheld computer; 3-D TopoQuads may be purchased by region.

Need a topo map really fast? Topographic maps are also available over the Internet. One site, www.TopoZone.com, has worked with the USGS to create an interactive topo map of the entire United States.

The site already has a good selection of individual maps, as well as the USGS 1:100,000, 1:25,000, and 1:24,000 scale map for the entire country. It will have topographic maps for Alaska (1:63,360) and Puerto Rico (1:20,000) available on its site shortly. To find the topo map you're looking for, simply type a place name in the search box and off you go. TopoZone says it will be adding lots of new features throughout the next year, so it should be a fun site to watch.

To make it easier to plot GPS coordinates, you might want to consider one of the latest specialized devices designed to do just that. The Yeoman Group makes the Yeoman XP1, a portable mouse for maps.

The XP1 takes data from a handheld GPS and electronically reads the map to tell you where you are and how far you have to go to reach your destination. It's a lot like using a two-button computer mouse. Simply connect the plotter to a GPS receiver, and a screen in the center of the mouse reads off the position in latitude and longitude.

By moving the mouse following the direction arrows, the device helps you position the mouse over your current location. You can use the XP1 in low-light situations, since the mouse display is LCD backlit. The XP1 weighs 1.7 pounds and uses 4 AA batteries. While I have yet to personally use this device, it has received several design awards in the United Kingdom and Germany. I also haven't seen it in retail outlets, but if you're interested, you can find more information on the company's website, which is www.yeomanuk.com.

As you can see, there's a lot to choose from in the GPS market, and more products are coming to market every day with more features, lighter weight, and lower prices. Technology being what it is, these units should continue to get smaller and cheaper in the near future.

GPS Dick Tracy Style

On the near horizon GPS receivers should continue to get smaller. Casio has already unveiled its first entry into the GPS market: the Casio GPS WristWatch, which went on sale in the summer of 1999 for around $400.

The production run was quite small and I never could get my hands on one in time for this book, so I can't tell you much about it, except the buttons are said to be painstakingly small. But still, it's a start, and rumor has it that the Swatch company will soon roll out its first GPS-enabled wristwatch as well. Increasingly innovative products and ways in which to use them are constantly emerging for your GPS receiver. By combining the Internet with portable computers and a GPS receiver, one California company hopes to revolutionize the way you search for services within a city's limits.

A California company, called Go2 Software, has created an entirely new system for combining web addresses with coordinates established by the World Geodetic System of 1984. These are the coordinates used by many receivers.

The company hosts hundreds of websites for companies like McDonalds and Starbucks. Their unique naming convention lets you use a portable device, such as a palmtop or laptop computer, a handheld personal digital assistant, a vehicle navigation system, or a cell phone, to get map directions by entering simple website names.

For example, you could enter Go2.coffee.com or Go2banks.com into a device equipped with an internal GPS chip or a device into which you can plug your GPS receiver. The device automatically knows where you are based on the GPS coordinates. It can then provide you with information about the nearest coffee shop or bank. It could even take you directly to their website or instantly deliver a map to your computer screen giving you directions to the nearest location. This sort of stuff is definitely coming, and it won't be long.

As far as topographic map technology, one of the most promising recent developments was the Shuttle Radar Topography Mission that took place in February of 2000. Sponsored by the National Imaging and Mapping Agency and NASA, this mission sent the Space Shuttle Endeavor on an eleven-day trek aimed at creating topographic maps of 80 percent of the earth's surface using radar technology.

Although NASA says it will take as long as eighteen months for the resulting maps to be available, it will be interesting to watch as the products emerge. They could definitely improve the quality and accuracy of the topographic maps you use with your GPS receiver to plan your treks.

What About SA?

Selective Availability was turned off by the U.S. government on May 1, 2000. This has significantly improved the accuracy of civilian GPS receivers.

How Can I Learn More?

It's a good idea to practice using all the functions of your GPS receiver before you ever go into the field. There are an amazing variety of ways to gain such experience. I made a few phone calls and discovered many learning opportunities in my town of Eugene, Oregon, that were cheap, or even free.

One local outdoor outfitter offered a free introductory class on GPS once a month on Saturday afternoons. The half-day course provided only a general overview of what GPS is and what the receivers can do, but it did allow participants to get their hands on a few different makes and models.

The local community college, on the other hand, offers an extensive sixteen-hour class (eight two-hour sessions) for only $32. It starts by teaching the basic map and compass skills necessary for backcountry land navigation, then moves on to an introduction of GPS.

The class includes field outings in which the instructor lays out a course on the ground and students determine the course coordinates using handheld GPS receivers. It also requires students to navigate a predetermined route using coordinates provided by an instructor. Students use GPS receivers alone and in conjunction with maps.

Not only does such a class provide education, practice in a controlled environment, and hands-on experience, but students also get the opportunity to use a variety of receivers throughout the course. By the time it's over, many know which receiver they want to buy and why. Then if you have a course certificate, a local outfitter offers a significant discount on the purchase of any equipment, including maps, compasses, GPS receivers, and map-reading tools.

With a $6 membership in the University of Oregon's outdoor club (open to any local citizen, whether you're a student or not), local residents can check out a GPS receiver for a couple of weeks at a time. The program offers occasional group lessons and orienteering activities, and allows you to gain experience with a variety of receivers before making a purchasing decision.

You may be able to save yourself some time and frustration by looking into such learning opportunities in your area. Start by calling some local sporting goods stores, the continuing education office at a local community college, the YMCA, or other community resources, and asking them if they are aware of any GPS classes in the area. It's a good way to learn in a safe environment with the oversight of an experienced instructor.

There's a lot to learn, a lot to do, and a lot of places to see. Happy navigating!

Part III

Survival

Be Prepared

This section provides the basics on the skills you might need if suddenly stranded, whether in the deep wilderness or only a few miles from home. But, far more important than any skill or device is your reasoning ability and attitude.

When faced with danger, we must stay calm and allow the reasoning process to develop. And never give up. Always keep trying. The worst challenge you will ever face has probably been overcome by someone before. People have endured incredible deprivation and lived to tell about it.

Our object here is to outline the skills and tell what action you should take so you don't ever have to see how much misery you can endure. Never go into territory without knowing which way you must go to get out. Always carry a compass and learn how to use it. Always dress for the worst conditions you might encounter and carry a basic survival kit. Finally, make sure someone knows where you have gone so searchers know where to start looking for you.

Learn how to make a fire with natural materials and build a shelter from the forest or plains. Learn to catch animals, fish, and find edible wild plants, and prepare them.

Almost anything can be made from natural objects if you have the skill. Outdoorsman John Sinclair made an excellent stone knife from the stones and shrubs growing around a cabin in northern Wisconsin. If you develop your skills and knowledge beforehand, getting stranded may be more interesting than exhausting.

Also learn to utilize what you have along. For instance, a brightly colored sleeping bag waved aloft is a noticeable signaling device, and the cosmetic mirror you have along can be used to reflect sunlight into the cabin of an aircraft to alert the pilot.

Making a Fire

A brightly burning campfire is a source of warmth and light. It is a cheerful companion and confidence builder, and it can be used to signal help, acquire and cook food, sterilize water, repel dangerous wild animals, and shape natural objects into useful tools. Making a fire should be the first order of business when lost or stranded.

In this modern age there are a great many people who have never built a fire at all, and a great many more who have never built one without fire-starting fluids. This is more difficult than might be realized and should be the first skill you acquire if you're going to be at risk of getting stranded in the backcountry. Practice building fires in widely different areas so you can learn to recognize burnable material. *Make very sure each fire is completely out before leaving it.*

No one should go into a wilderness area without some means of starting a fire. I carry a plastic 35mm film container full of stick matches. I have to break them off to fit, but this small container will hold two dozen matches if the ends are alternated. It can be carried in any pocket and will keep the matches dry even if I fall in the water. I have several of these containers, and recently discovered one that had been in a coat pocket for a year. The matches still worked perfectly.

Fire Starters

Place a small piece of emery cloth in the container to strike matches on. Take at least 200 matches; also take at least four candles along. Use a match to light the candle, then use the candle to light tinder to start a fire. Candles will also furnish light and can be used for light cooking. If you set the candle in a container, it can be recycled.

Waterproof camping matches are available from camping supply outlets, or you can make your own by coating kitchen matches with paraffin.

An excellent fire starter for survivors is a device called a magnesium fire starter or "metal match." It consists of a block of magnesium and a flint insert. A small pile of magnesium is scraped from the block with a knife. Then the insert is scraped with the knife to produce fat, hot sparks that will ignite the magnesium. This device will work even if it gets wet, and the burning magnesium will ignite any dry tinder. A disposable cigarette lighter is also a good fire starter, and most will give more than 1,000 lights. They are light in weight and inexpensive and will work even after they get wet.

Primitive Methods

People do get lost, however, and for one reason or another have no fire-making materials along, or they quickly use up their supply of matches. Therefore, every outdoorsperson should practice making a fire by primitive methods. If nothing else, finding out how demanding and time consuming starting a fire without matches is, will remind the traveler to carry a good supply of matches on every backcountry trip.

The bow-and-drill method of starting a fire is the most versatile (see figures 12-1 and 12-2). It should be learned by anyone who is at risk of getting lost or stranded. The raw materials are at hand wherever trees grow. The string for the bow can be made from a boot lace or even coated wire from a vehicle's wiring harness. This method is far from easy. Don't wait until you are stranded to learn how it's done.

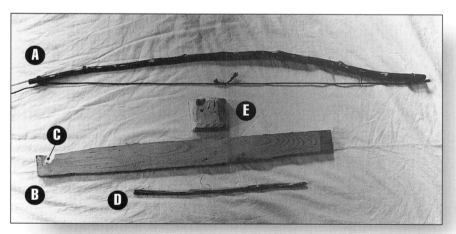

Figure 12-1
....

Bow and drill fire starter. The bow (A) should be 36" in length. The fire board (B) should be 30" in length. However, the fire hole (C) should be put in on the flat side about 24" from a chosen end. The drill (D) is 18" in length, and the socket (E), which holds the drill, is 3" in width.

Figure 12-2

Make a fire using a bow and drill.

I spent about eight hours of concentrated activity before getting a fire burning from a bow and drill. But now that the device is made, I can usually get a fire going in a half hour or so. A new hole has to be drilled in the fire board every two or three lights because the drill will wear out the original hole. The fire drill has to be reshaped quite often also.

Here's how I made mine: Using a large belt knife, I split a 3-foot length of white spruce limb to make the fire board. It is about 1 inch thick and 3 inches wide. Next I found a dead seasoned maple sapling about ⅝ inch in diameter and shaped it into a fire drill 18 inches long. The bottom end was tapered to about a 45 degree angle, and the top of the drill was simply rounded off and made as smooth as possible. The drill headpiece was a dead, seasoned piece of maple log about 3 inches square. A socket was gouged into the center of the headpiece to fit the top end of the drill. I lubricated it with earwax and oil from beside my nose.

Working carefully I used the point of the knife to drill a hole in the fire board that would fit the taper on the fire drill. Directly underneath the hole, a V-shaped notch was formed to hold the tinder.

A hard maple limb with a natural bow shape made a 36-inch-long bow. I used my boot laces for a bow string. Notches were cut near each end of the bow to keep the laces from slipping. The string has to be tied fairly snug but not too tight because the fire drill is wrapped in the string.

I placed the tapered point of the drill in the hole in the fire board, held the top with the headpiece, and sawed the bow back and forth to spin the drill. The drill soon milled the hole to a snug fit, and shortly thereafter smoke started coming from the hole. I stopped then and went looking for tinder.

I found a dead cedar tree and made tinder from the inner bark. I shredded it until it was so light and fluffy it would almost float in the air. I packed the tinder into the V notch under the hole in the fire board. Finally after several hours of drilling, reshaping the drill and its seat in the fire board, and trying again, I got the tinder smoldering and blew it into a flame.

To sum up: This method of making a fire is far from easy or quick, but it definitely works. Best of all, the components can be built from natural materials, and if no knife is at hand, they probably could be made with a sharp rock or a piece of broken glass.

Using What's at Hand

Fires can be started with a magnifying glass if the sun is nearly overhead and shining brightly. You can carry a small magnifying glass along on an expedition for just this purpose. I have a "bull's-eye" magnifying glass that will start a fire in a minute or less when good tinder is available (see figure 12-3). But with any type of magnifying glass, you have to move the lens back and forth until you've adjusted the sunlight shining through the glass to a small brilliant dot. Situate the dot to shine on a tight ball of tinder and it will quickly start smoking. Hold the tinder in one hand and the magnifying glass in the other so you can blow on the tinder after it starts smoldering. This is not as easy as it might sound, and you should practice this procedure beforehand.

A telephoto lens from a camera also can be used to start a fire (figure 12-4). Remove the lens from the camera and use the same procedure as you did with the magnifying glass. Lenses taken from binoculars and telescopic rifle sights also can be put together to produce a magnifying glass to start a fire.

We have created fire with both smokeless and black powder, a tin can lid, and a magnifying glass. We shaped the lid to a bowl shape and fastened it on a stump so that it protruded over the edge to cut down on heat conduction. We filled the lid with powder and directed the bull's-eye of light on the metal under the powder. In a few seconds to a few minutes, the powder would ignite with a noticeable "poof" into a significant flame.

Discarded bottles and decorative glass figurines have, reportedly, acci-

Figure 12-3

A bull's-eye magnifying glass and natural tinders will quickly start a fire.

Figure 12-4

A telephoto lens and natural tinder will also start a fire.

dentally started fires that burned forests and dwellings by concentrating the sun's rays on burnable material. If no magnifying glass is at hand, experiment with other materials.

If sparks are the only way to get a fire started, try out, maybe after dark when sparks are easier to see, any metal or rocks at hand to see if they will produce a hot spark, as some will. Accidental fires have been started by a combination of volatile fuel and sparks from casually thrown rocks.

I have tried to get a fire burning without success from sparks made with flint and steel; from firing a gun fueled with smokeless, modern powder; with a fire plough; and with a fire thong. I don't believe they are workable ways for a survivor to get a fire burning, even though they are recommended in many books.

Tinder

Regardless of the method used for making a fire, however, it won't be successful without good tinder. Learn to recognize this material before you get stranded. Use the inner bark from dead trees, dry small twigs shredded between the fingers, dead grass shredded between the fingers, mouse nests, downy feathers, wasps nests, dried evergreen needles, dry moss, cattail fluff, punky material from inside dead elderberry stalks, and dried animal dung, which all make good tinder.

If the surrounding forest is wet, finding dry tinder is more difficult. Try the wispy bark from birch trees that can be gathered without a knife. It is impregnated with oil and doesn't absorb moisture. The inner bark from dead standing trees and the inner core of a rotting stump that can be kicked apart might have dry tinder. Don't forget that the paper in your wallet, the cuffs of your shirt, your handkerchief, or even the top of your shirt tail can be shredded to make tinder when the surrounding area is wet.

Firewood

Good tinder is very important to start the fire, but good dry fuel to keep it burning is equally as important. Be sure the fuel is piled so the tinder can be placed underneath it. Tiny dry twigs piled tepee fashion will quickly catch fire if placed over burning tinder. Have some larger twigs at hand to put on the fire. After branches an inch or so in diameter are burning, there will be time to gather larger pieces for fuel. Gradually increase the size until logs 6 inches or more in diameter will burn. They will hold a fire for hours. If they can't be cut up in short lengths, just push the ends into the fire, let them burn off, and push up another length.

Sometimes it is easier to make up fuzz sticks than to find small twigs. Take a short length of twig an inch or so in diameter and whittle it toward one end so a shaving is produced. But don't cut the shaving off. Leave it on the branch so that the end result looks like a shuttlecock. Lean the fuzz sticks against each other, tepee fashion, and place the burning tinder underneath them.

You will fuel most survival fires with whatever wood is nearby. Seldom will you have a choice of woods to use. Soft woods, such as dry evergreen wood, burn fast and produce sparks, but often this is all you have. Dry aspen, dry alders, and maple tree limbs all make very good wood that will last for hours. A fire will burn overnight if you lay two green logs across the burning campfire so that flames rise between them. If they get a good start before the rest of the dry wood burns up, they will smolder all night.

When it is difficult to get a fire burning, be sure it doesn't go out while you are sleeping or during a rainstorm. Always keep at least one coal alive. At night bank the fire first with ashes and then a layer of dirt so the coals will stay alive. If it rains, cover the banked fire with bark, a flat stone, or whatever waterproof covering is at hand. When you move, carry a live coal in a tin can or bark container. Cover the coal with a 1-inch-thick layer of ashes, and it will not burn the container or die for as long as forty-eight hours. Rotten but dry wood also will hold a fire for a long time without bursting into flame. It can be carried along and blown into flame when needed

Finding Water

Water is easy to find on most of the remote places left on earth. The far north has snow and ice in winter and plenty of surface water in summer. Jungles are well watered, and many plains areas have rivers and potholes full of water.

Most of this surface water is contaminated and should be treated or boiled before it is ingested. Be sure to take water purifying tablets along if you will be flying over or traveling through remote areas. But if you don't have tablets, the water should be boiled at least ten minutes before being consumed. Only in a dire emergency should untreated surface water be consumed, and then a doctor should be advised after you reach civilization again.

Desert and arid regions are a different matter. In the desert dying of thirst is a distinct possibility, and every desert traveler should develop their water finding skills before going into one.

A person in the desert who did not exert him- or herself could live from two to three days with temperatures 100 degrees or more without water. At 50 to 75 degrees a person can live up to ten days without water. In the desert an inactive person can live for five days if he or she has two quarts of water per day. On the same amount of water at 75 degrees, the same person should live ten days. In cool temperatures a person can be mildly active and live on two quarts per day indefinitely.

Fortunately water is found nearly everywhere; even on the driest desert, it sometimes can be located. If such dire emergency arose that you would have to try to walk out from the desert without water and without a particular destination in mind, head for the roughest ground or for visible vegetation. If you can get to hills, there might be water near their base. A dry creek bed also might have water somewhere running underground. Palm trees, cattails, grass, bushes, and greasewood can grow only where water is found near the surface.

Animal trails probably lead to water in the desert. Birds also can point out a waterhole. They often circle over a water source, or their flight patterns are often directly toward water. Animals might scratch at the surface where water is close to the surface, and sometimes honey bees or other insects will gather on moist ground.

If you have a piece of plastic along on your person, or in a stranded vehicle or airplane, a solar still can be made (see figure 13-1). Dig a pit in the lowest land available, about 2 feet deep and 3 feet in diameter, or as large as your sheet of plastic will cover. Leave enough slack so that you can place a rock in the center of the plastic to pull it down to a cone shape. But the first step after digging the pit is to place a tin can, a shoe or hat, or another object that will hold water at the center of the bowl. Now place the plastic across the top of the pit and hold it around the rim with sand or rock. If the ground around the pit holds any moisture, it will evaporate out and condense on the plastic. Then it will run down the sides of the cone to drip into the container under the plastic.

Up to three pints of water per day can be extracted from some desert soils this way. Try to remove the plastic only once per day, just before dark. If any other source of moisture is available, even the pulp, stems, or leaves from plants, it can be placed under the plastic. The plant juice will evaporate and condense again into water also. A solar still can be used to convert swamp or alkali water, or even the solution from the radiator of a disabled vehicle, to pure drinking water. Dig a trench under the plastic and fill it with the contaminated water.

Don't forget you can also recycle your own urine in this way.

When water is available, conserve it as much as possible by moving only during the coolest part of the day. Talk very little and don't smoke or eat unless your food is full of moisture. Breathe through the nose and keep your clothing on because this will cut down the rate of perspiration somewhat. When you rest in the shade, try to make a bed about 1 foot above the sand. It can be 30 degrees cooler a foot above the ground. If you can't rest above the ground, dig down into the sand about 2 feet.

The human body can store water for short periods to some extent. Drink all the water you can before you set out on an arid journey. It is possible to saturate the tissues enough so that you can go a day or two without serious dehydration. Some travelers place a pebble or two in their mouths to keep the saliva flowing so the mouth doesn't feel too dry.

Watch also for water holes built in extremely remote locations for desert sheep. They are called guzzlers. Also, if you are lucky, you might spot a windmill, or cattle or sheep watering pond.

The prickly pear cactus grows in great quantities and its pad and fruit

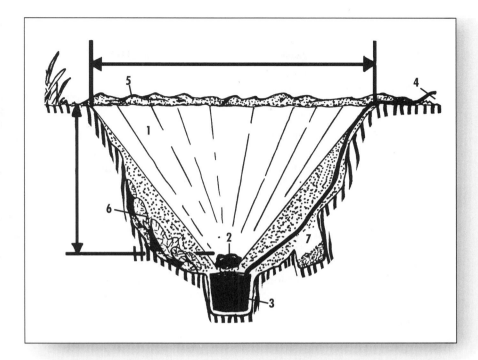

Figure 13-1

Desert solar still.

Legend:

1. Sheet of wettable plastic, 6-foot diameter.

2. Smooth, fist-sized rock for forming cone of plastic.

3. Pail, jar, can, or cone of soil, plastic, or canvas to catch water.

4. Drinking tube, ¼-inch plastic, about 5 feet long (desirable but not necessary).

5. Soil to weight plastic sheet and seal space. A good closure is important.

6. Line hole with broken cacti or other succulents.

7. If nonpotable water is available, dig a soaking trough around inside of hole. Carefully fill the trough to prevent impure water from running down and contaminating the water-catching container.

both contain large amounts of juice. Try not to get scratched; its thorns are long and wicked. Also the stalks of mescal, sotol, Spanish bayonet, and barrel cactus can be cut and drained of their juices for emergency use. Cut the pulp into pieces and suck on them.

Collect rainwater in hollows in the ground coated with plastic or cloth. Sop up water from puddles with clothing or handkerchiefs. Quickly dam up any nearby trenches to form pools.

Dew can be heavy, even on the desert on occasion. It will collect on stones, vegetation, or metal surfaces, such as auto bodies or airplane wings. Mop it up with a cloth and squeeze it out into a container. If there are nearby trees, the dew collects on the surface of the leaves. Mop it up also. When tall grass or brush is wet with dew, tie rags around your ankles and walk through the dew soaked vegetation. Wring out the rags in a container afterward.

In arid regions where grass is growing and has been growing for many years atop rocks, there will be a layer of muck or mud below the grass. Dig into this muck to look for water. There might be water just underground. Dig out the earth filler in cracks and let the water run out.

In arid regions keep an eye out for cottonwood trees. Find the largest cottonwoods. They are almost a sure indicator of water. Dig in any near-by low places for water. White brush growth is also a sure indicator of water; mesquite growth probably indicates a dry area.

Anytime you can find nonpoisonous plants or trees with green leaves, you can use the plastic bags from your survival kit to create a "leaf still" that will supply drinking water (see figure 13-2). Without cutting the leaves from the plant, loosely wind or tie as many as possible into a bunch. Aerate a plastic bag to expand it to a round shape. Then slide the bag over the bunch and adjust it so the plastic doesn't touch the leaves. Place a small clean pebble in the bag, tie it at the top, and shape the bag so the pebble creates a small reservoir at the bottom to collect the moisture.

When the sun starts shining, it will draw water vapor from the leaves. The vapor will suspend or condense in droplets on the inside of the bag. Eventually the moisture will condense into larger drops and trickle down the sides of the bag to the reservoir. Remove the bag carefully and extract the moisture. Don't leave it overnight without collecting the water, or its moisture might be reabsorbed into the leaves. A surprising amount of water can be collected this way, but create as many stills as you can to have a reliable source of water. The leaves in the bags will have to be changed each day.

You can extract water from cut leaves, water plants, pieces of cactus, or even damp soil with a "stump still" (figure 13-3) made with a plastic bag. Place the leaves or plant pieces in the bottom of a bag and set it on

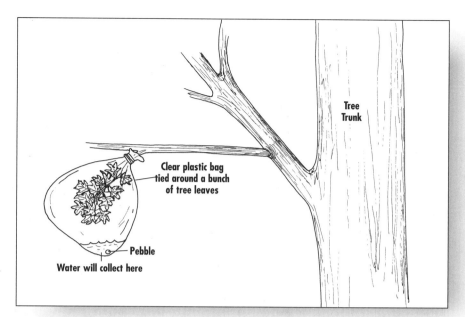

Figure 13-2
....

Leaf still.

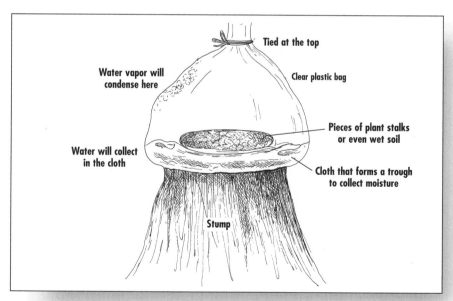

Figure 13-3
....

Stump still.

a stump, rock, or earth mound. Use your "handy cloth," a T-shirt, or a few pairs of socks to create a trough inside the bag, which is around the outside of the stump. Tie the top of the bag so it is airtight and suspend it from a tree branch. The water that condenses will run down the sides of the plastic bag to be soaked up by the cloth. The cloth can be wrung out into a container, or the moisture sucked out directly into your mouth. The stump still can be left overnight without losing the collected water.

Streams, rivers, and lakes flow in great profusion in most northern and mountainous areas, and water usually can be found without much trouble. If possible, it should be boiled for ten minutes. Water, even in remote places, can be contaminated with a half dozen diseases that are carried by animals. But if you can find a spring that bubbles up from the ground, the water will probably be pure.

Stagnant water, even if it is badly contaminated with algae or mud, can be made potable by straining it through a filter made by tying a trouser leg at its bottom, partially filling the leg full of clean sand, and then pouring the water into the leg so it must run through the sand. Catch it in a container. It also should be boiled before drinking. Several layers of cloth will also strain most particles of contamination from the water, and sometimes you can dig a hole into the bank a few yards inland from the shore of a pond and find water that is clean. It also should be boiled if possible.

Sometimes a vessel can be hollowed out of wood, or a bowl-shaped stone can be found that will hold enough water to boil. Of course if you have no choice, drink the cleanest, coldest water you can find.

It is possible that you will be caught along a seacoast in a survival situation without fresh water. Often water that is drinkable can be found back away from the seacoast by digging into the sand. If you don't dig too deeply, the slightly salty water is palatable. Dig mud holes to catch rain water.

Where snow and ice are present, no one will die of thirst. Eat snow if you can't melt it. Melt it only if you have a plentiful supply of fuel. It takes 10 inches of snow to make 1 inch of water. Eating snow and ice will not make your mouth sore if you only eat small amounts at one time.

Finding Food

S tarving to death is not an immediate problem. Most of us can go weeks without eating if necessary. In fact, for many people, after about three days, the sensation of hunger leaves and doesn't return for a week or more. But food is an important morale builder, as well as fuel for the muscles and brain, and as soon as adequate shelter is constructed most people will start looking for sustenance.

If you are stranded along a watercourse, look for clams, crayfish, and fish. Fish can be caught by hook and line, speared, or caught in traps. Fish hooks can be fashioned from twigs, fish skeletons, small animal bones, or thorns (see figure 14-1). A gorge-type fish hook can be made by just sharpening a small twig on each end. Make a groove at the center for fastening the line.

Fishing line is somewhat harder to obtain. Some clothing can be unraveled enough to produce a fish line. A leather belt can be cut into thin laces and used for fishing line, and the inner bark of some trees, when cut into strips and knotted together, is strong enough to make fishing line. Wire from a vehicle or airplane also might be used for line.

A fish spear (figure 14-2) can be made from forest materials. We made spears for spearing suckers when I was young by just cutting a green hardwood sapling about 8 feet long and 2 inches in diameter. Cut a V notch on the lowest end and sharpen both points very well. Barbs are not necessary on a survival-type fish spear, because the fish is speared and then held to the bottom of the lake until you can reach down and grab it with your hands. A crotched stick (figure 14-2) also can be used to pin fish to the bottom where the bottom is firm.

After the spear is made, position yourself on a rock or log overlooking the shallows and stay as still as possible. When a fish comes into view, slowly slide the spear into the water. Get as close to the fish as you can without actually touching it. Aim low to allow for refraction of the water, and then made a hard thrust.

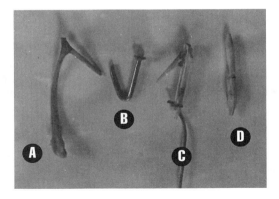

Figure 14-1

Fish hooks can be made of many different materials:

(A) Bird bones carved into fish hook shape.

(B) A nail.

(C) Fish hook made from a thorn.

(D) Gorge made from a branch.

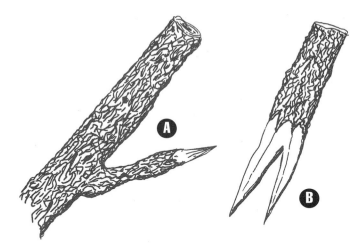

Figure 14-2

(A) Crotched stick.

(B) Carved hand spear.

If you've made a torch, try night spearing. Some fish are actually attracted to light, and others just ignore it. At night they are often in shallow water feeding and offer good targets. Fish also can be clubbed or killed by dropping stones on them when they are in very shallow water.

Be sure to put out a few fish traps also (see figure 14-3). The traps can be made from rocks or with stakes pounded into the bottom of the lake. The shallow water section of a shoreline point is a good location for the traps, as is the inlet or outlet from the lake. These traps work well in streams also. Sometimes fish can be driven downstream into a trap.

Minnows are abundant in most lakes, streams, and rivers. Often they will supply more pounds of food than larger fish because they are much easier to get. Make a minnow trap (figure 14-4) by finding a hollow driftwood log, 1 to 3 feet long. Close off one end with branches or rocks. Then put fish guts or other bait in the end of the log nearest the branches. Place the log where you have seen minnows in the shallows and weight it down with rocks so that it sinks. Then find a birch tree or other type of tree with peelable bark and remove a section about 15 inches by

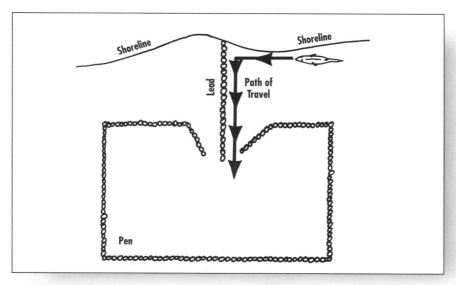

Figure 14-3

Fish move along the shoreline after dark. When they encounter the lead, they turn toward deep water and are confined in the pen. Use logs or stones for the lead and pen. They have to project above the waterline. The lead should be about 10 feet long, if possible. Build the pen as large as you can make it.

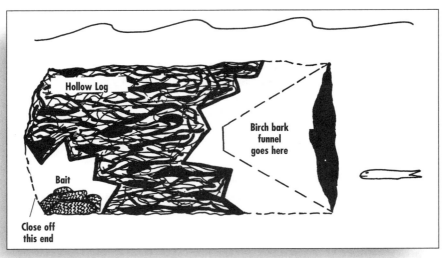

Figure 14-4
....

A minnow and small fish trap.

20 inches and roll it into a funnel. The small end of the funnel should be about 2 inches in diameter. Push the funnel into the log with the small end inward. A few such traps placed in good locations can catch two to ten pounds of minnows a day.

Minnows may also be caught with a net from a jacket (see figure 14-5).

Strip the waste matter from their intestines by squeezing them, and then swallow them whole. They can be eaten raw or baked on a hot rock.

You can snare larger fish if you have some light wire or string along. Make a noose in the line, and when you see a resting fish, approach it very carefully and work the noose over its head, back of the gills. Then jerk it quickly.

Some fish can be grabbed by hand if you move slowly enough until your hand is under the belly. Then throw the fish out on the bank or grab it in the gills.

Watch eagles and hawks also. Sometimes you might be able to scare them away from their kill of a large fish.

In winter chop a hole in the ice and make a sharp gaff (figure 14-6) whittled from a tree branch to gig fish when they swim under the hole in the ice. Leave the gaff in the water until the fish is positioned directly above the hook. Then jerk it upward to drive the point of the gaff into the fish's belly. Keep lifting it to bring the fish up through the hole in the ice. A wooden gaff can also be used to catch fish from open water.

Figure 14-5

Pounds of minnows can be caught in one scoop with a net from a jacket. Minnows can keep you from starving to death when big fish are hard to catch.

ice

hole in ice

Figure 14-6

Wooden fish gaff made from a tree branch.

In many places rabbits and squirrels, along with gophers and chipmunks, porcupine, skunks, marmot, and other small animals, can be harvested by many different methods. Grouse, ducks, geese, crows, gulls, and all the birds of prey are edible, as are small songbirds.

Gophers and ground squirrels, tree squirrels, and cottontail rabbits can be found in ground burrows or in hollow trees. Where the ground is soft, you can dig the animals out with a sharp stick used as a shovel. If some means of carrying water is at hand, you can pour water down the burrow until you flood the animal out. If you want to reach the animal with a stick, use a twisting stick made from a forked tree branch. Push the stick against the animal and turn it to wind up the hair. Then pull the animal out where you can kill it with another club.

A snare (figure 14-7) can be used to catch everything from a mouse to a moose, if the right sized wire is at hand. A snare is simply a length of wire, rope, cable, or even cord made of plant fibers that has been formed into a "hangman's noose" by tying a small loop in one end of the string and pushing the other end of the cord through it, forming a loop that will tighten up when pulled on. The loop is adjusted to the right size and set in an animal's trail, so that when it walks down the trail it will

Figure 14-7

If you have the material, make up from forty to one hundred snares to set around your camp. It will require this many to keep you in food, especially during summer when animals do not follow trails most of the time.

push its head through the loop, but it won't be able to get its legs and body through. As it continues to advance, the loop will tighten up and strangle the animal or tighten around its body and detain it until the survivor arrives.

Most snares are set to catch cottontail rabbits or snowshoe hares. These animals are abundant in almost every environment and have regular travel routes that can be noticed easily when there is snow, but also can be found in summer by looking for narrow trails through underbrush or berry patches. The snare is usually set where the trail passes between two saplings or other natural restrictions that will guide the animal into the snare. Also the snare must be secured to a substantial sapling or other anchor to hold the animal after it is caught. Jackrabbits are found on the plains or in some deserts. They do not follow trails as much as the other species, but they can be caught in snares placed where they follow animal trails along dry ditches or to waterholes.

Big game can be snared, also, if stout wire or cable is available. In remote areas of Wisconsin, backwoods folk snared hundreds of whitetail deer with barbed wire fencing a few decades back. They followed a deer trail until it passed between two closely spaced trees. Then they placed a log between the trees so the animal had to duck its head to pass under it. Next they formed a snare from the wire and located the loop of the snare so the deer's head ducking under the cross log would enter the snare. You can adapt this method to catch small moose, small elk, antelope, or caribou. In arid regions snares should be set near waterholes in places where animals are guided to a specific location by natural vegetation or topography.

You can also snare birds and animals by pulling on a noose when they are in the right position. Prop up the snare, attach a long cord, and conceal yourself nearby. When the animal or bird is in the right position, pull the cord tight.

Make a box trap (figure 14-8) from forest materials. The trap is made so that when the animal enters to get the bait, a door will fall down behind it and confine it to the box.

A box trap can be made of logs or stakes. Cut stakes about 18 inches long and sharpen them at one end. Drive them into the ground about an inch apart to form a rectangle 10 inches wide and 18 inches long. Close off one end and roof the tops with a log or with several smaller poles tied to the sidewalls.

Fit the open end with a door made from materials at the site. The door must slide up and down in the four end stakes of the sidewalls. Tie a string to the top of the door and run it to the back of the trap. Fit this end with a trigger that will hold the door up when the string is tight, but drop it when the animal bites on the bait.

Survival   **133**

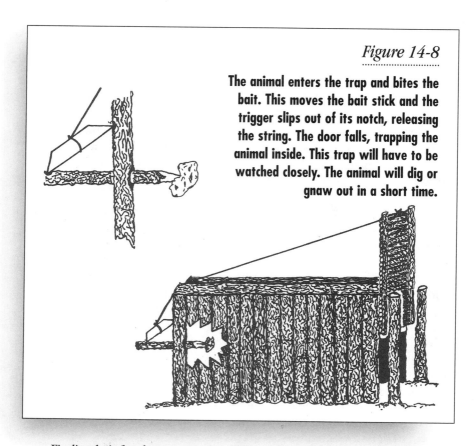

Figure 14-8

The animal enters the trap and bites the bait. This moves the bait stick and the trigger slips out of its notch, releasing the string. The door falls, trapping the animal inside. This trap will have to be watched closely. The animal will dig or gnaw out in a short time.

Finding bait for the trap can be difficult. Small animals usually have plenty of food, but they crave salt, and you can produce a salt bait from your own urine. First find a porous piece of wood small enough to be used as bait for a box trap. Place the piece of wood on a small bowl-shaped depression in a rock that will hold liquid. Urinate on this piece of wood so that the wood is soaking in urine. The salt in your urine will impregnate the wood, and after a few days, it will be salty enough to attract small animals. Fasten the piece of wood to the trigger of the trap.

If you are trying to survive in the forested regions of North America, look for a beaver pond. Beaver populations have exploded—their ponds dot almost all wilderness areas. One large beaver can feed a man for days. Moreover, their ponds will certainly contain fish, clams, crayfish, and frogs and might be a watering hole for nearby deer or moose, which also can be used for food.

You can get a beaver with a club. First look along the edges for signs of beaver cutting. If you see a tree that is partly cut off and the cutting looks like it is freshly made, the beaver will probably return to finish cutting it off that evening. Make a blind from tree branches or whatever is at hand and wait for the beaver to come out of the water. Be sure you are downwind of the animal and have a stout heavy club. Beaver have strong skulls and bodies, and it takes a tremendous wallop to disable one. Wait until it is clear of the water, get between it and the pond, and run it down. Beaver cannot move very fast on land.

If they won't come out on the bank, find the weakest part of the dam and pull it apart. A tremendous sluice of water will gush out. Stand by it with a club to kill any fish or muskrats that might ride this spillway out of the pond.

Long before the water is all out of the dam, the beaver will try to repair it. They will swim up to the hole in the dam and examine it, then disappear and return shortly with material to start fixing it. Hide nearby with a club or spear. If you don't get a beaver this way, wait until the water is low enough so that you can wade out to the beavers' lodge. Chase the beaver out by pushing a stick down into the lodge through the air hole opening in the top. When they come out, have a club or spear ready. They also might swim out to earth dens in the banks where you can dig them out. Beaver can be snared also if you have some stout wire along.

In the spring and early summer, the young beaver will not come out. But they will start mewing when the old ones leave. If you hear this sound, tear the lodge apart and get them. They will be at least as big as rabbits and are excellent eating. These methods are illegal in most states, but if your life is in danger, they must be used.

In the far north in the spring, look for a wetland where ducks and geese may be nesting. The eggs, young birds, and also the adult birds might be easy to get because you can catch the birds on the nest. Adult geese are respectable adversaries and could even break your arm unless you are armed with a stout club. They also can bite hard enough to draw blood.

When waterfowl are roosting in large flocks, you should be able to kill one or two by throwing a club into their midst. Also if you happen to find the waterfowl during the molting season, they cannot fly. They can be run down and dispatched.

In remote areas Franklin's grouse, spruce grouse, and ruffed grouse are unwary enough to allow you to get close enough to them to kill them with a club. In the spring watch on the ground at the base of a clump of willows or the base of a tree for grouse and ptarmigan nests. You might be able to get the hen and her eggs.

According to records would-be survivors have starved to death from what might be called "plate fright." They just couldn't eat what was available to them. Human beings can digest insects, snakes, lizards, grubs found under tree bark, and most other creatures that move about on the earth. Don't turn down any food in a survival situation. In early morning earthworms can sometimes be found on top of the ground. Squeeze them so they expel the contents of their innards and eat them raw or baked on a hot rock.

Cattails might be found in forests, plains, and even desert environments because they grow wherever areas of swampy wetlands are located. Cattails can furnish food all year around. In early spring the young cattails are growing up. Pull them up and eat the tender white base of the plants. Later in the season, early July in the upper Midwest, the bloom spikes will be growing up. Near the top of the spike a miniature "ear of corn" grows. Eventually it will become the cattail, but at this point it will look like a pencil-sized green tube with a yellow center. Snap off these tubes, peel the husks away, and boil or roast them. They taste like corn on the cob. When they mature enough to bloom, pollen hangs thickly on the blossoms. It too is edible and will add a "corn" taste and attractive yellow color to flour or fish chowder. Gather it by shaking the blossoms over a container, such as a paper bag or a hat.

Cattail roots look like brown rope, and they seem to twine in every direction. They can be peeled, roasted, and eaten. At intervals along the roots, there will be new shoots growing. They are pure white and resemble a huge animal's tooth. Snap them off and eat them raw or cooked.

Cactus can furnish food also. If you can break open the stalk, the inner pulp of some species is edible, either raw or roasted. Furthermore, some bear fruits that are edible. In fact there are no poisonous cactus species. If you can reduce the cactus to food-sized bits; it can safely be eaten. To make sure you can safely consume cactus or any other plant, except mushrooms, follow this procedure:

First squeeze some juice onto the skin of your upper underarm. Wait ten minutes. If there is no reaction, taste a small amount without swallowing. Wait ten minutes. If there still is no reaction, eat a small amount and then wait five hours without eating or drinking anything to see if you have a digestive reaction. If you don't, it should be edible. If you do get a strong reaction, drink hot water to induce vomiting or swallow a paste of water and white wood ashes to neutralize the effects.

Practice finding and preparing edible wild plants and catching fish and animals before going out into the wild.

Making a Survival Camp

I n all but a few instances the most self-serving procedure is to made a bivouac camp and stay put after you realize you are lost. Transportation is so rapid and search efforts are so intense and well executed in this modern age that it is nearly always senseless to move. Spend your energy improving camp, putting out signaling devices, and finding food.

If you can get a significant fire going and have a plentiful supply of fuel, a lean-to will usually be the best choice of shelter. With this combination you can withstand any temperature on the globe and be downright cozy in most situations. To build a lean-to, find two trees about 6 to 8 feet apart that have sturdy limbs about 6 feet above the ground. Remove all nearby limbs except one on the same side of each tree. Locate a sturdy sapling about 10 feet long and lay it across the limbs to form the ridgepole. Find at least six other 10-foot saplings and evenly space them at right angles to the ridge to form a roof. Weave flexible twigs or pine boughs among the roof poles to form a weather-tight roof (see figure 15-1). If there is enough material at hand, close in the ends also.

Figure 15-1

Building a lean-to shelter. Cut boughs and weave them between the roof poles to make a tight roof.

Build your fire about 6 feet from the front of the lean-to. As long as you can keep the fire going, this camp will be warm.

In the northern regions the evergreen trees are the best friend a lost person ever had. Their thick boughs can be used to make a warm comfortable bed and to cover a pole framework to make a shelter (see figures 15-2 and 15-3). Moreover, the air temperature under a thick stand is actually up to ten degrees higher than in open areas. Furthermore, the thick evergreen trees usually break the wind, which considerably reduces the chill factor caused by moving air.

Therefore, if you are forced to spend the night in the woods in cold weather, by all means go into the thickest evergreen stand you can find to make your survival camp. If you have a knife or hatchet the work will be much easier, but limbs can be broken by hand. Especially in cold weather, limbs will readily snap off.

Figure 15-2

Build a pole and evergreen bough shelter starting with a downed tree. Such a shelter can be built without tools by breaking the branches off.

Figure 15-3

Cover a pole frame with pine boughs. When done with care, such a shelter can be made almost windproof.

There are downed trees in every forest. Find one that has been broken off a few feet above the ground but has not separated from the stump. Break off the branches on the underside of the trunk so that it will form a ridge pole. Leave the side branches attached and bring in the others to make a tent-shaped framework (figure 15-4). Cover this framework with evergreen boughs woven tightly together, make a floor of evergreen boughs, and you have a dandy shelter that will withstand snow and wind. Also, put a 6-inch layer of pine boughs on the ground inside the shelter for a bed.

For a quick overnight tree shelter, look for a spruce or pine tree with limbs growing nearly to the ground. Break off the branches on the downwind side of the tree to make an opening large enough so you can sit with your back against the tree (see figure 15-5). Weave the branches that you cut off into the other branches to make it even tighter than it is naturally.

Also, put a thick layer of boughs on the ground to sit on so that the moisture and cold from the ground will not reach your hips and legs. You can rest fully clothed in such a shelter during the dark hours. Practice building these shelters before you get lost. Then it will be an automatic task.

Figure 15-4
....
A-frame shelter.

Figure 15-5

A tree shelter.

In the plains or arctic regions you may get caught in open country with night coming on and a blizzard blowing up. Immediately look for whatever natural shelter is available. Find the lee side of a ridge, a gully, or the downwind side of a huge boulder, and make a shelter from the snow. Snow is usually hard packed by the wind in plain areas and can readily be utilized for a shelter (see figure 15-6). Find a snowdrift at least 4 feet deep. They are usually located on the lee side of a huge rock, ridge, or stand of thick vegetation. Use your feet, a board, a forked stick, or whatever is at hand to create an opening in the snow. Collect sagebrush or whatever dry vegetation is at hand to create a lining to lie or sit on.

If you have your survival kit along, the tarp can be used for a roof and the plastic bags used to cover the ground to keep your clothing dry. Space blankets can be spread under and over your body to retain warmth.

If no natural windbreak is available, make a trench shelter (see figure 15-7) in the snow. I have made these shelters using just my feet for a digging tool. I make them about 8 feet long and 3 feet wide. They are formed at right angles to the wind so the sides of the trench break the wind. If grass, cattails, sagebrush, or evergreen boughs are available to make a bed in the shelter, it will positively keep you from freezing to death. Also, if available, find enough vegetation to put a roof over the

Figure 15-6
....

This shelter was hollowed out of a hard snowbank. It is also lined with evergreen branches.

trench. Then the blowing snow will cover the top and make it even warmer. If you can't cover the top, push the snow you've removed from the trench into a ridge at least 6 feet upwind from the trench. This ridge will act as a snow fence and keep most of the drifting snow from blowing into the hole.

A large fallen log or rock pile can form one side of a survival shelter also. Lay poles on the log or rocks to form a lean-to roof. Cover the roof with evergreen boughs, grass, sagebrush, willow brush, weeds, or whatever is available. Make it only as large as needed. The smaller the shelter, the warmer it will be if no other heat is available except body heat.

Building a survival shelter is quite strenuous work, and it is easy to try to move so fast that you perspire heavily. This exertion can cause your body to chill badly when you finish and stop moving about. Discipline yourself to move slowly to prevent heavy perspiration, especially if you can't start a fire when you have finished.

If you are following a stream or river through the wilderness, keep an eye out for abandoned beaver lodges. Sometimes they are built far from the main channel because the area was flooded by the dam when the beaver built it. After the beaver have left and the dam has been washed out, the beaver house may be left high and dry. Enlarge the entrance so

Figure 15-7

A trench shelter can keep you from freezing to death, but be careful not to work up a sweat making it.

you can get in it, and it will form a completely tight and weatherproof shelter for sleeping. Abandoned beaver ponds invariably have a good stand of dead poles lying around. You can use them for shelter frames or for burning.

In plains areas sagebrush sometimes grows large and sturdy enough to use as materials for making a shelter. Usually the densest growth is in gullies and ravines. Here the sides of the gully will also help break the wind and make the shelter more snug. If the stalks of sagebrush are not sturdy enough to use for a frame, pile rocks or dirt clods to form a trench that you can sit or lie down in. Pile sagebrush around and over it to make it more secure.

Look for a cave or overhanging bank in plains or mountainous or hilly terrain; it makes an excellent shelter, as does a partial cave if the sides can be covered with tree branches or other vegetation.

Although the Inuit lived in igloos in the harshest climate on the globe, igloos are not survival shelters. It is far quicker and easier just to burrow into a hard snowbank for the shelter than to make an igloo, unless you have the skill and tools.

A great many people are stranded in their cars each year during blizzards or because they get stuck in the sand or mud. Almost everybody who dies from such an incident left the vehicle and struck out on foot. Sometimes they had no clear idea of where they were going. It is far better to stay with your vehicle in nearly all instances. When it is cold, keep warm by running the engine periodically, but be sure the exhaust pipe is not plugged by snow or mud; also, keep a window open a crack so you won't be overcome by carbon monoxide poisoning.

If you run out of gas, you might keep warmer outside the car because the metal body of an automobile conducts heat away very rapidly. You will need a wind-tight shelter to survive very long in cold weather. Often there are materials or clothing in the car that can be used to make a lean-to type of shelter. Floor mats, seat covers, trunk liners, seats, and the hood or trunk doors can be removed and used as part of the shelter. You can make a warm bed by using the cushions from the front and rear seats. Cut each one open and remove most of the stuffing material. The hollow formed will fit the human body. The foam material you remove can be used to plug up drafty holes in the shelter. Nearby trees, brush, fence posts, or road signs can be used to make sides for a shelter. If you can survive for three or four days, help will surely arrive.

People have expired after their car became stuck in the sand in the desert. Usually they died of thirst and heat prostration after they left their vehicle and tried to walk out. It is far better to stay with the vehicle. Sleep inside the car at night and burrow under the car into the sand during the daytime. If you can't dig under a vehicle to escape the sun's rays, consider making a double-roofed shelter to rest in during the heat of the day. To do so find a natural depression or dig a trench about 2 feet deep, 3 feet wide and 8 feet long. Pile the sand nearby to use later. Roof over the trench with sticks, brush, plastic, or a tarp, if you have two tarps. Create a 12-inch-high sandbank around the edges of the roof and place a tarp over this to form a second roof. Conserve your water supply by not sweating. If you work on the vehicle to try to get it unstuck, do this at night, late afternoon, or early morning. Don't move anymore than you have to during the heat of the day.

You can use a large boulder, overhanging bank, dry streambed, or even the shady side of a cactus to shelter yourself from the sun. If you can't find shade, try to lay or sit on some object several inches above the sand because it will be as much as twenty degrees cooler than it is on the surface of the sand.

Small airplanes have been forced to land in the desert also. During the hot part of the day, the airplane will be too warm to stay in. However, the fuselage and wings will create shade, and this can be enhanced by using plastic or cloth material from the airplane draped over the wings to make a lean-to to turn away the sun's rays. Digging into the sand even in the shelter will help you stay cool. At night the interior of the airplane is an excellent shelter, in part because it will be safe from intrusion by poisonous snakes.

In cold climates the interior of the airplane is nearly the worst possible shelter because it will conduct heat away so rapidly. It will be mandatory to make a shelter outside the plane to avoid freezing to death.

Most airplanes that fly in the far north carry survival items along. A survival kit will usually include a tent or plastic tarp to use as a tent, space blankets, matches, flares, fish line and hooks, and dried food. You can use a parachute to make a lean-to shelter or as a ground cloth.

If you haven't any survival materials, fashion a shelter from the available natural materials as explained. The gasoline and oil and battery can be used to make a fire and for signaling.

144

Signaling for Help

No one should go into remote territory without leaving word of where they are going and when they are expected back. If you walk out, leave a note in the vehicle when you are expected back. If you fly, be sure to file a flight report. Boaters also can leave word at a boat landing or with any available person.

Several devices are available for signaling in an emergency. A well-equipped survival kit will include a flare gun and flares, as well as a signaling mirror and whistle. Many survival kits also contain colored dye or colored cloth that can be laid out to make signals. Directions for using these devices are included with the kit, and there are further instructions in this chapter.

A cellular phone is an excellent addition to your survival equipment. If you have one along, and the phone is working, rescuers can be quickly alerted. They don't preclude the basic equipment and knowledge every backcountry traveler should have, though. For instance, even after being alerted, rescuers still might have to search for you, and physical signaling devices will be needed.

Furthermore, the batteries might be "numbed" by cold weather so they don't activate the transmitter, or the unit might be soaked from rain or by being dunked in a lake and won't transmit. Dirt might contaminate the device or it might be damaged from a fall.

Protect the phone by wrapping it in several layers of clothing placed inside a sealed plastic bag (if a commercial shockproof, waterproof container will add too much weight to your backpack). If the batteries are numbed by cold weather, place them next to your skin to warm them. In heavily forested areas or deep mountain valleys, the phone might not be able to transmit. You must then move to a clearing or to a hilltop. Do this before using up the battery power.

Figure 16-1

A piece of wood kept wet will reflect light and can be used for a signaling device. A piece of glass coated with mud on one side may be used in this way also.

A great many people have been lost without any survival kit to aid them. They must improvise. Fire is the most noticeable signal that a survivor has at his disposal. The flame from fire is readily visible at night.

But be sure to build the fire where it can be seen: on an island, a lakeshore, a hilltop, in a large clearing, or even on a floating log or raft out in a lake.

Smoke can be seen for many miles in the daytime, and most of the forested regions of North America are watched over by rangers in fire-spotting towers or by regular flights of airplanes whenever the ground is snow free. A fire 6 feet in diameter, well smothered with green boughs, grass, or water plants will give off enough smoke to be spotted by fire spotters or searchers. Then help will arrive in a hurry.

If you can't keep a fire going continuously, lay the fire with tinder and fuel wood and cover it with birch bark, or whatever is available to keep it from getting damp. Then when you hear an airplane, light the fire. Three large fires spaced 100 feet apart in a triangular shape will signal an airplane that you need help.

Figure 16-2

Waving a brightly colored jacket on the end of a stick will catch a pilot's eye. This is also good in the mountains to signal searchers.

Many times you can use an isolated, dead tree standing in a clearing or along a lakeshore as a signal tree. If the tree has dead branches so that it will burn well, pile grass, small dead branches, or dried moss in the bottom limbs and have it ready to set on fire. The flames will climb up the tree and make a torch visible for many miles. Again, the best time to light it is after you hear an aircraft.

Fire can be used to blacken a clearing, burn off a small island, or blacken tree trunks or rocks to make a signal to searchers. Anything you can do to the surroundings to indicate your presence will attract a search plane. After an airplane has spotted you, smoke will show the pilot in what direction the wind is blowing, so he or she will know how to approach the landing. If possible, have a landing site marked.

Signal mirrors also can be contrived from the materials at hand. A piece of broken glass covered on one side with dark mud will make a usable mirror. A tin can lid can be polished until it is like a mirror, and a log slab kept wet from a nearby puddle can be used as a mirror to reflect light toward an overhead airplane (see figure 16-1). In winter a slab of ice can be used for a mirror. Keep the mirror moving so that it will attract the pilot's attention.

When snow covers the ground, stamp out the letters SOS, filling in the letters with pine boughs or other dark materials. Make the letters at least 20 feet high if you can. Letters laid out in a general east-west pattern will cast a shadow and be much more visible from the air.

Pilots will fly low enough over lakes and rivers to look for tracks on sandbars. If you encounter sandbars, make tracks and figures in the sand as large as you can. Particularly scratch out SOS signals as large as you can make them.

If a tool is at hand to remove the bark from trees, peel several trees in a group because this will make an eye-catching signal from the land or air. Rocks or logs piled in the pattern of a cross will also attract attention. Make the cross about 20 to 30 feet long, if possible.

If you have some brightly colored clothing that can be spared,

Figure 16-3

Be sure to learn this hand signal: It means "I need help." All pilots will recognize this signal. Do not just hold one hand up because that means "I don't need help."

148

climb a tree and tie it in the top, where it will wave in the wind. Waving bright colored paper or clothing with your hands on the end of a stick (figure 16-2) will also attract attention. At night torches waved around in the air are very noticeable.

Shooting also can attract attention if done at the right time. Wait until after dark when the hunting has ended for the day, then fire three evenly spaced shots. This is the universal distress signal. Then stay quiet and wait for answering shots or shouts. If you get an answer, walk toward the sounds. But if you don't hear any more answers, and it looks like you can't walk out, stop and stay in one place until help arrives or until the next morning.

In deep wilderness shooting isn't likely to attract attention and it will only waste the ammunition you might need to get food. The exception would be if a search party was looking for you and was close enough that you would hear them.

Whistling can attract attention and can be kept up longer than shouting. A commercial whistle makes the most noise, but many people can "shepherd whistle" also. Do this by placing the thumb and forefinger together in the roof of the mouth. Then blow a quick puff of air. You will produce a sound almost as loud as a commercial whistle.

Pounding on a hollow log, a rock, or any metal object, of course, will make considerable noise, and this can be kept up for a long time to guide any nearby rescuers.

Signaling for help is largely a matter of common sense. Keep a clear head and utilize whatever materials are available. The first day or two that you are lost, sound signals will likely be the most effective. After that an aircraft search will likely be initiated. Then sight signals are most apt to be spotted.

Be sure to learn the hand signal for communicating with an airplane pilot that means "I need help." The distress or "I need help" signal is to hold both hands above your head (see figure 16-3). Don't hold up just one hand because this means "I don't need help."

Above all keep a clear head, make your camp or trail as visible as possible, and make as much noise or create as many visual signals as possible. Do this and without a doubt you will soon be rescued.

Walking Out

Death, mental or physical illness, or just plain forgetfulness might result in your being stranded in a remote area without any means back home. Walking out might be mandatory.

But before you start walking, ask yourself a few questions: Are you physically able to walk out? Can you make snowshoes or fashion skis to get through the deep snow? Do you have adequate clothing? Can you withstand the insects? Can you find food or water? Do you know the way?

After you decide to walk out, take your time deciding what to take along. If you have a choice between taking a sleeping bag or shelter, take the shelter. You can sleep in your clothes. The tent will keep you from getting wet, which has possible fatal complications in cold weather.

Matches or some fire-starting device should not be overlooked. If candles can be found, they are excellent for starting fires along with fulfilling their intended task of giving off some light. By all means take along spare socks if available. Don't forget a knife or hatchet.

If no packsack is available, tie up the items in a piece of cloth or canvas and sling it over your shoulder like Depression-era hobos did (see figure 17-1).

First locate a landmark before setting out. In heavily timbered country, this can be a faraway bluff, a lake, or an exceptionally large tree or rocky outcrop. It often is impossible to walk directly to a landmark. You may have to skirt swamps or go around lakes. To keep from getting off the trail, sight on some close-by object, such as a tree. Walk to it, then pick out another and walk to it. If this is done carefully, you will get back to your original route without losing track of it.

When the sun is shining, of course, it will indicate the general direction. Walking directly into the rising sun will take you in an easterly direction, directly into the setting sun in a westerly direction. If you want

Figure 17-1
....

Carry your clothes over your shoulder tied to a stick.

to walk east during the middle of the day, the sun should be over your right shoulder; you're traveling a westerly route if the sun is over your left shoulder. When you walk south, the noonday sun will be shining in your face.

Night travel is an option in some areas. The insects might be so bad at night that you can't sleep and elect to travel. During the full or nearly full moon, this is quite possible even in wilderness territory. In the desert night might be the best time to travel to escape the hot sun.

The moon also rises in the east and sets in the west, so use it to determine your direction of travel. But actual travel routes will still have to be determined by lining up objects and walking to them. Most nights you can't see very far ahead and must use nearby landmarks. It would, of course, be very foolish to travel in strange, rugged territory on a dark night. When traveling at night, if you stop to rest, make a pointer to show where you came from and where you were going. Otherwise, the next morning you may have forgotten which tree or landmark you were walking toward or even in which direction you were going.

Of course no one should go into strange territory without a compass and at least a rudimentary idea of how to use it. Know also in which direction the broadest target is likely to be found. A road or large settle-

Figure 17-2
....

Stop early enough to make camp and cook food to keep up your strength.

ment would be a much wiser goal to aim at than an outpost, even though the outpost is much closer.

For instance, imagine that you are lost in the deep forest east of Red Lake, Ontario, Canada. You know that Highway 105 lies west and offers broad lines to strike out for. It is nearly 40 miles away and will probably take you five to eight days to reach because you will have to skirt numerous lakes. You also know that an outpost is located at Cat Lake only about 10 miles away, and another outpost is found at Slate Falls, about 15 miles distance. The outposts are closer, but if you miscalculate, you will be wandering in a huge expanse of trackless wilderness. Which should you choose? Without a second thought, strike out for Highway 105 directly west.

As mentioned in the signaling section, while you are walking out, try to stay ready to signal any airplane that might fly over. Airplanes fly regularly in many remote areas and might see you if you are in an open spot ready to signal.

Once you start moving, resist the temptation to rush toward your objective. Walk at a moderate or slow pace and stop long before dark to make camp and cook food to keep up your strength (see figure 17-2). Keep safety foremost in mind. Never step over anything you can walk around; never step on anything you can step over. Be extremely careful when crossing rivers and streams. If there isn't a safe crossing where you first encounter the river, follow it until you find one, or make a raft. If you encounter an extremely large lake or river, it is likely to be frequented by people sooner or later. Make camp and wait.

A river or chain of lakes is about the easiest route to follow in winter when frozen over. The snow cover is usually much shallower on ice than it is on the land, and it offers a definite highway that eventually will lead somewhere. But even in the far north, ice can be treacherous. Swiftly running water, unseen from the top, can cause the ice to be very thin over rapids or where the normal flow is compressed between two banks. A thick snow cover at the shoreline can insulate so well that the water doesn't freeze very thickly. Sometimes it is impossible to tell if ice is thick enough to be safe by looking at it.

But on the positive side, most ice in the north will hold up a person. You can usually tell if the ice is too thin by probing ahead of you with a sturdy stick. If you have a good knife along, lash it securely to a stick about 4 feet long and 2 inches thick. Keep jabbing the ice ahead of you as you walk. If the knife blade goes through, the ice is too thin to hold you up.

Some northwoods travelers carry a long, lightweight pole with them while walking on the ice. You hold the pole at the center so if you fall through, it will keep you from going down under the ice. But having participated in long treks over the ice, I know that after a day or two without any problems, most hikers will forget about the pole. It is too much trouble to carry. With no pole, your sheath knife is the best friend you have, because if you fall through in a place where it is too deep to touch bottom, you might not be able to get back up on the ice again unless you have a handhold.

If this happens, remove your sheath knife from its sheath very carefully so that you don't drop it. Your life might now depend on it. Grip it securely, hold yourself as far up on the ice as you can, and then drive the point of the knife into the ice. Use this as an anchor point to pull yourself back up on the surface of the ice.

If the weather is so cold that the snow is dry, roll immediately in the snow to remove as much water as you can from your clothing. Then get to shore and build a fire. If you can't build a fire, the only chance you have of surviving is to keep moving until your clothing dries out. Otherwise you will almost certainly die of hypothermia.

If you encounter a large river while walking out, follow the river. It will probably lead to help eventually. Moreover, you are very likely to encounter other people or see aircraft along a good sized river. Personally I would not try to walk any farther than the river unless I was sure that help was close by. I would either make a raft and float down it or make camp and stay put until someone came along. But like most other aspects of survival, this would be a judgment call.

Glaciers and large lake ice can have deep cracks filled with snow. If you fall in one, you might not get back out. About the only way to know if a snow-filled crack is in your path is to keep probing the snow ahead with a pole. If it is summer and the glacier ice is melting, water will be running everywhere, even making ditches too deep to cross. Travel from midnight to midmorning if possible to avoid most of the running water. Snowslides are also a hazard to travelers in the far north mountain or glacier terrain. If you get caught in a snowslide, try to swim to the top as if you were swimming in water.

In winter and fall the desert might be a friendly place to travel. The temperature is agreeable, and usually you can sight a distant landmark to keep oriented. A range of mountains in the distance, for instance, might be the only landmark you will need for days. The chief danger might be from flash floods or from the nights actually getting so cold that you will suffer from hypothermia. Try to rest in a cave or depression out of the wind but high enough so that a flash flood during the night will not catch you unaware.

Conversely, in the summer the desert becomes a hell hole, so hot and dry that without water a person can die trying to walk in the heat of the day. The best chance you have is to drink all the water you can, carry all that you can, and walk only during the cool part of the morning or late in the afternoon. The desert can be cooler after dark, but you might fall over a cliff or even walk in a circle without the sun to guide you. If you happen to have a flashlight, or if the moon is bright and you have a compass or trail to follow, night travel is an alternative.

Try not to walk in soft sand by traveling on ridges or troughs between dunes. Take good care of your feet by dumping sand out of your shoes regularly. If a sandstorm comes up, lie down with your back to the wind and cover your face with a handkerchief or other cloth. If you get caught out in the open in the heat of the sun, dig into the sand as far as you can and cover your body with sand. This can keep you twenty degrees cooler than the ambient temperature.

Snowshoes, sandshoes, or bog shoes can help a survivor stranded in deep snow, loose sand, or soft mud. They can make the bearing area of the foot large enough so it is possible to traverse otherwise impassable terrain. Pieces of board, sections of flat metal from an airplane, or several layers of cloth or canvas soaked in water and folded into a rectangle and allowed to freeze hard can make usable shoes. Tree limbs, driftwood, or small saplings are most apt to be used to make survival shoes.

Survival shoes (figure 17-3) made like miniature ladders, about 1 foot wide and 3 or 4 feet long, will function as well as more elaborate designs

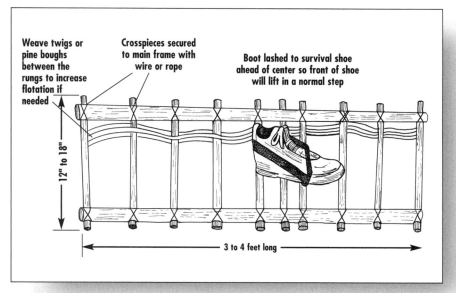

Figure 17-3

Survival shoes are for use in snow, primarily, but are also useful for traversing bogs or soft sand.

and are easier to construct. Use approximately 2-inch diameter saplings for the side frames, with 1-inch diameter crosspieces. If dead but seasoned saplings are at hand, use them to save weight. Wire from your survival kit can be used for fastening the "rungs" to the side frames. If you don't have wire, consider strips of clothing, seat upholstery, leather laces cut from any spare boots, or even tree bark or roots. To increase flotation, weave twigs or pine boughs or even cloth or canvas between the cross pieces. The foot is lashed so the survival shoe will lift in a normal walking step. Lashings must be flexible, but strong. Possibly the best material you have along will be your bootlace. If you have to use them, then substitute strips of cloth or bark to lace up your boots.

For Novice Desert Travelers: Advice from a Desert Rat

If you are a novice to desert travel follow this advice, and you will never die of thirst or heat exhaustion in the desert. First, make sure someone knows where you are going and when you will return. Next, if feasible, take along a cell phone or radio so you can report your emergency.

If you drive into remote areas in a vehicle, take along an extra spare tire, a spare fan belt, and a roll of duct tape for repairing radiator hoses. Watch your radiator temperature and stop to let it cool if it starts rising too much. Drive slowly and carefully to avoid hitting rocks, and don't cross creek beds or gullies without checking to see if the sand is too soft to drive on. Don't back off the roadway to turn around without checking for the same reason. Even so be sure you have jacks and blocks for raising the vehicle so you can get something solid under the wheels if you do get stuck in the sand. A portable come-along hoist and at least 50 feet of tow chain is well worth carrying. Next consider that, for whatever reason, if you get stranded you may not be rescued for up to three days. Besides a basic survival kit, have a shelter tarp, a sleeping bag, and five gallons of water for each person.

If you are hiking, imitate the desert creatures and only move during cool hours of the day. Try to take a cell phone or a GPS unit. Never travel alone and make sure someone knows where you are going and when you are expected back. Have good up-to-date maps and study them beforehand to plan your route; if you do wander from the trail, know in what direction and how far you must travel to find water holes, ranch houses, or roads. Besides your survival gear, carry at least a gallon of water, and if you do get lost and find water, stay there until help arrives.

Getting Out by River

If a river flows by your camp, you have a ready-made route to follow out. Follow any river and eventually you'll get to a place where you can find help. The river is also a means of transportation if you can make a raft.

Along almost every large stream or river, you will find material for building a log raft (figure 18-1). Sometimes only two logs are needed to make a raft. Unless you are far upstream from an unnavigable part of the river, chances are the best thing you can do is make as comfortable a camp as possible and wait for someone to come along. This probably will not take long in most areas because people are floating and motoring on every large river during the ice-free months. Some rivers are as busy as highways.

In some places fallen but sound logs are strewn about in good numbers. Once you find the material for building the raft, reduce the logs to the right size. You will find that you need to use smaller logs due to the weight of larger ones. This can be done with fire if you don't have an ax or saw on hand. About the easiest way to build a raft is to lay the poles side by side and then lay another smaller log across and tie them together with rope. If you do not have rope, the logs can be held together with notched sticks.

Be sure to build the raft large enough to hold up everything you have as cargo. The bigger the better. Build the raft rectangular rather than square as it will be easier to steer. After tying the first layer of logs together, you will need to build a deck over them so that you can stay dry. Also you will have to find or make a pole or sweep in order to steer the raft. Travel using the raft only when it is light enough to see ahead. Even then stay close to the shoreline so you can land in a hurry if noise

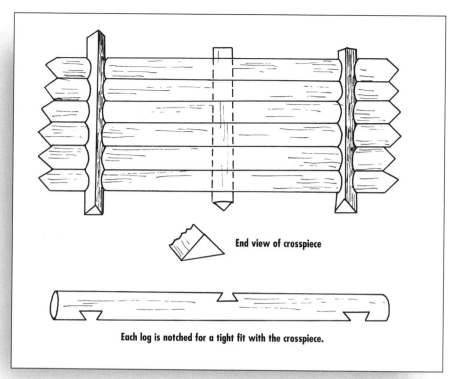

End view of crosspiece

Each log is notched for a tight fit with the crosspiece.

Figure 18-1

Making a raft.

ahead indicates rapids or a gorge. Never enter unknown rapids without getting out and walking ahead looking out for danger. Usually you can line the raft through rapids by letting it down on a rope. Another possibility is to take it apart and let it float down one log at a time. You can choose to build another below the dangerous area. Of course you could also take the chance of letting it float through, hoping it will make it, catching it below the rapids.

Usually it will be quicker and safer to walk out, rather than try to build a raft and float out. But there are clear exceptions: If you find a large stream or river with a good current but very little, if any, rapids or very shallow water, and you have more than 100 miles to go, then a raft might be feasible, especially if material for building one is close to the river.

Appendix I
Common U.S. Map Symbols

Topographic Map Symbols			
Primary highway		Gravel beach or glacial moraine	
Secondary highway		Woods (green)	
Light-duty road		Scrub (green)	
Unimproved road		Orchard (green)	
Trail		Rock bare or awash	*
Bridge		Group of rocks bare or awash	
Building: small; large		Sunken rock	+
Cemetery: small; large		Intermittent stream	
Standard gauge single track; station		Disappearing stream	
Abandoned track		Large falls; large rapids	
Power transmission line; pole; tower		Masonry dam	
Telephone or telegraph line		Intermittent lake or pond	
Quarry or open pit mine	X	Dry lake	
Mine tunnel or cave entrance		Water well; spring or seep	
Sand or mud area, dunes or shifting sand		Marsh or swamp	

Appendix II
GPS Resources

DeLorme
Two DeLorme Drive
Yarmouth, ME 04096
(207) 846-7000
www.delorme.com

Garmin
1200 East 151st Street
Olathe, KS 66062
(913) 397-8200
www.garmin.com

Lowrance Electronics
12000 E. Skelly Drive
Tulsa, OK 74128-2486
(800) 324-1356
www.lowrance.com

Magellan Systems Corporation
960 Overland Court
San Dimas, CA 91773
(909) 394-5000
www.magellangps.com

Maptech
655 Portsmouth Avenue
Greenland, NH 03840
1-888-433-8500
www.maptech.com

Navitrak
603 Argus Road, Suite 201
Oakville, Ontario
Canada L6J 6G6
1-800-257-6766
www.navitrak.com

The Yeoman Group
The Shipyard
Bath Road
Lymington
Hants SO41 9YL UK
www.yeomanuk.com

Appendix III
Surface-to-Air
Emergency Signals

The traditional eighteen International Surface-to-Air Emergency Signals were often not well known to pilots. So they recently have been replaced with the following five easily memorized signals by the International Convention on Civil Aviation:

V
I require assistance.

X
I require medical assistance.

N
No.

 Yes.

 Proceeding in this direction.

Air-to-Ground Signals
Consist of the following:

Will drop message: gun motor three times

Received message: rock plane, side to side

Affirmative: "nod" plane

Negative: "wag" plane

Fire or other location here: circle three times

Appendix IV

Basic Survival Gear

ost people know they shouldn't venture into a wilderness without suitable clothing. They should always wear sturdy boots, tough, tear-resistant clothing, and a suitable hat. Fortunately there are many suppliers of such clothing. Some suppliers of top quality leather outdoor boots are Rocky, Wolverine, Danner, Browning, Justin, and Cabela's. The Sorrel and LaCrosse companies make suitable winter weather boots with a leather top and rubber bottom. Winter weather boots should always have a removable liner so they can be dried between outings.

At present my favorite pair of leather outdoor boots is a pair of Rocky "Super Brutes." I wear blue jeans in summer, mostly wear Cabela's Camo clothing in fall and spring, and wool trousers in winter. My favorite outer jackets are made by Carhart and Browning. My favorite shirts are "stone washed" canvas in summer, fleece or wool in winter. These are available from Cabela's and WalMart, among others. I wear baseball style hats in summer and wool stocking caps, trooper, or fur hats in winter. Wool mittens and gloves or leather chopper mittens with liners are good cold weather choices, as are cotton socks in summer and wool socks in winter. I spend most of my time in the north woods, so these items are mostly tested in a cool climate. A knowledgeable desert traveler wears sturdy boots; lightweight, loose-fitting outer clothing; and a hat with a wide brim.

There are dozens of catalogs filled with dandy little products that you could find use for in a survival camp, but don't try to take too much. If a fanny pack weighs more than about two pounds, you probably won't carry it every time you walk out into the forest or desert, as you should. When making up your survival kit, keep in mind that, primarily, you need to drink, sleep, and keep from freezing or overheating in order to sustain life. You probably won't die without food or miscellaneous medical supplies before being rescued. There are many other items that will make a survival situation more tolerable, however. Here's what I carry in a fanny pack to sustain one person for *three* days:

Three-Day Pack

1. Two space blankets.

2. Four square feet of aluminum foil.

3. A plastic film canister containing fifty strike-anywhere matches.

4. A compass and a police whistle. I also have a pin-on compass.

5. Two clear plastic kitchen bags and two oversize leaf bags. Orange bags are more apt to be seen by rescuers.

6. A small, commercial first aid kit containing Band-Aids and Dristan tablets.

7. Water purification tablets.

8. A sturdy candle.

9. Small flashlight that uses AA batteries.

10. Two quarters, two dimes, and two nickels.

11. A lightweight knife with a 3-inch blade. I also always carry a pocketknife.

12. Insect repellent.

13. Orange marking tape.

14. A quart of water, but in the desert, at least a gallon.

15. Food is optional . . . if you don't mind the weight.

Use the space blankets to wrap up in or push both inside a large plastic bag to make a waterproof sleeping bag. The plastic bags will make a solar or leaf still, or serve as a ground cloth to sit or lay on, or an emergency raincoat or gear cover or to keep mosquitoes at bay. You can use the aluminum foil to make a signaling mirror, drinking cup, cooking pot, and numerous other items. Glue a piece of sandpaper inside the lid of the film canister to strike the matches on. Use the candle for light and for sustaining a fire long enough to start kindling. In addition to these fire starters, I have a magnesium fire starter and a canister of matches buttoned into each of my fall and winter jackets so I can't forget them. Turn one battery in the flashlight backward to prevent accidental discharge. The coins are for a pay phone if you encounter one. You can use the marking tape for making the trail to guide rescuers, and it can be used as rope for making shelters and has numerous other applications.

Make sure the knife is of good quality steel. My pocketknife is a Schrade, "Old Timer" series, and my daypack knife is a "Twistlock" by Cold Steel Company. Likewise, your compass must be absolutely reliable. My main compass is a "Sportsman" model by Michaels of Oregon. Other companies make reliable gear also, but stick to a well-known supplier. This is no place for cut-rate products.

Seven-Day Pack

A second pack, to sustain one person for a week or more, should contain, in addition to the three-day pack items:

16. A small aluminum cooking pot.

17. A week's supply of water purifier tablets or a PUR water purifier pump.

18. A spool of 40 nylon fish line, a packet of fish hooks, and a half dozen sinkers.

19. A signaling mirror.

20. A lightweight, bright blue down sleeping bag.

21. Enough freeze-dried food to supply 10,000 calories (five day's supply).

22. Nine square feet of aluminum foil.

23. Two Bic cigarette lighters, a packet of tinder made of 00 steel wool, interspersed with hemp rope fibers.

24. A hand-operated pencil sharpener, pencil, and small notepad.

25. A 10" by 10" section of 6 mm plastic tarp.

26. One-hundred feet of 32-gauge steel wire for rabbit and squirrel snares.

27. Twenty-five feet of quarter-inch nylon rope.

28. A folding camp saw.

29. An outdoor first-aid kit as listed in Appendix V.

Use the fish line for tying components of a shelter together, repairing clothing, snaring and making traps, and fishing. Leave messages to guide rescuers on the paper. Use the tinder with the magnesium fire starter to create a flame. Tinder is meant to be used up first; keep the matches for later. Be sure to pull the steel wool fibers apart before striking the spark, and when it glows, blow hard to start a flame. You can make tinder with the hand-operated pencil sharpener faster and better than any knife. Find a dead, seasoned twig that will fit or can be shaved to fit and "sharpen" it.

The tarp can serve as a shelter, and the rope may be used for hanging the shelter or a dozen other tasks around the survival camp. The saw is for cutting poles for a shelter frame, cutting firewood, or clearing away vegetation to make a camp or a signaling icon.

Appendix V
The Outdoor
First-Aid Kit

State-of-the-art dressings, including such things as 2nd Skin and various size of gauze, wound closure tapes, and nonprescrip-tion medications will allow any hiker or hunter to construct a very useful first aid kit for general outdoor use.

Very often treatments can be improvised with other items on hand, but prior planning and the inclusion of these items in your kit will provide you with the best that modern medical science can offer.

Quantity	Item
2 pkg.	Coverstrip closures, ¼" x 3" (3/pkg.)
1	Spenco 2nd Skin Dressing Kit
1	Bulb-irrigating syringe
5 pkg.	Nu-Gauze, high absorbent, sterile, two-ply, 3" x 3" pkg.
1	Surgipad, sterile, 8" x 10"
2	Elastomull, sterile roller gauze, 4" x 162"
2	Elastomull, sterile roller gauze, 2½" x 162"
10	Coverlet Bandage Strips, 1" x 3"
1	Tape, hypoallergenic, ½" x 10 yd.
1	Hydrocortisone cream, .5%, 1 oz. tube (allergic skin)

1	Triple antibiotic ointment, 1 oz. tube (prevents infection)
1	Hibiclens Surgical Scrub, 4 oz. (prevents infection)
1	Dibucaine ointment, 1%, 1 oz. tube (local pain relief)
1	Tetrahydrozoline ophthalmic drops (eye irritation)
1	Starr Optic Drops, ½ oz. bottle (ear pain, wax)
1	Micronazole Cream, 2%, ½ oz. tube (fungal infection)
24	Actifed tablets (decongestant)
24	Mobigesic tablets (pain, fever, inflammation)
24	Meclizine 25 mg tab (nausea, motion sickness prevention)
2	Ammonia inhalants (stimulant)
24	Benadryl 25 mg cap (antihistamine)
10	Bisacodyl 5 mg (constipation)
25	Diasorb (diarrhea)
25	Dimacid (antacid)
2 pkg.	Q-Tips, sterile, two per package
1	Extractor kit (snake bite, sting, wound care)
6	1 oz. vials for repackaging tablets, salves, or liquids
1	Over-pak container to make up a convenient kit

Consideration should be given to a dental kit. Several are commercially available through backpacking and outdoor outfitters. As a minimum a small bottle of oil of cloves can serve as a topical toothache treatment, or you can carry a tube of toothache gel. A fever thermometer should be included on trips. People wearing contact lenses should carry a suction cup or rubber pincher device to aid in their removal.

Appendix VI
Ten Steps for Survival

1 Remove yourself from danger, such as vehicle explosions, precarious footing, or hazardous waterways.

2 Find a campsite and build a basic shelter.

3 Build a campfire. Besides providing warmth, a campfire has a calming effect and promotes confidence.

4 Find water. Treat all surface water or boil it for ten minutes.

5 Start signaling. Put out commercial signals, display bright cloth signals, and make tracks in the sand and mud and otherwise change the natural appearance of your surroundings so they will be noticeable from the air and land. Keep a smoky fire burning. Make all the noise you can. Keep flashing your signal mirror in all directions even if you don't hear or see help.

6 Look for edible plants. You can eat grass, cattail roots, insects, inner pine bark, berries, reindeer moss, plantain, violets, arrowhead roots, acorns, and most other plants. For safety, try very small amounts at first.

7 Try to catch fish or animals for food. Fish, clams, crayfish, frogs, minnows, rabbits, and rodents are most likely to be nearby. Set snares or construct traps for rabbits and rodents.

8 Move in seven days. If you're not rescued in a week, consider moving camp to a more visible location.

9 Find the four directions. Remember the sun rises in the east and sets in the west and so does the moon. Stick two three-foot-high sticks in the ground and sight across them at a star. If the star rises, you're looking east. If it moves to the left, you're looking north.

10 When it's time to start walking out, walk in a straight line by sighting on landmarks. In almost every region of North America you should find help within ten days. Go at a reasonable pace and stop early enough to make camp.

Common Map and Compass Terms

Agonic line: A line or zero declination. At any point along this imaginary line, the compass will point true north.

Aiming off: The navigator aims to the right or left of his objective, rather than straight at it. This creates a purposeful error in a known direction, which helps in targeting the objective. See pages 44-46 for details.

Attack point: A point on the map that is easy to identify on land (hilltop, road junction, railroad crossing, etc.). Same as a "checkpoint."

Back bearing: Also called reciprocal bearing. It is the opposite direction from which you came. Or 180 degrees plus or minus your forward bearing.

Baseline: A handrail that's used as a reference line for positioning when afield. The navigator works on one side or the other of the baseline. A return bearing is plotted to the baseline, which is then followed "home."

Base plate: The ruled plastic base of an orienteering compass.

Bearing: A direction, in degrees, from where you are to where you want to go. Technically, it's a horizontal angle measured from north to your direction of travel.

Cardinal points: The primary directions—north, east, south, west.

Compasses: See chapter 3 for compass types and their differences.

Compass rose: The 360 degrees of the compass circle.

Contour interval: The difference in elevation (usually above sea level) from one contour line to another.

Contour lines: Light brown lines on a map that indicate height above sea level.

Declination: The direction in which the compass needle points. More accurately, it's the angular difference between true north and magnetic north, or between grid north and magnetic north (called "grid declination"). Expressed in degrees east or west of the agonic line.

Declination diagram: A diagram in the legend of topographic maps that gives the value of the area declination.

Doghouse: A slang term for the printed arrow inside the housing of orienteering compasses. When the "dog" is in the "house" (magnetic needle inside printed arrow of housing), the compass is properly oriented.

Direction-of-travel arrow: An arrow inscribed on the plastic base plate of orienteering compasses points towards your objective when the compass is properly oriented (needle centered in the doghouse).

GPS (global positioning system): An electronic unit that receives positioning information off orbiting satellites. With a civilian model GPS, you can locate your position anywhere on earth in a matter of minutes. Accuracy is 100 meters or less.

Grid lines: Interconnecting lines superimposed over the face of topographic maps.

Grid north: The direction the grid lines point with respect to true north.

Handrail: A topographic feature that you can follow to your objective, such as a road, river, creek, power line, trail, or lakeshore.

Housing: The part of the compass which contains the magnetic needle.

Index: A master map that contains information for ordering topographical maps. Also the place on a compass where the bearing is read.

Intercardinal points: Intermediate compass points—northeast, southeast, southwest, northwest.

Latitude: The north/south measurement (given in degrees) of a position perpendicular to the earth's polar axis.

Longitude: An east/west measurement of position (given in degrees) relative to the Prime Meridian located in Greenwich, England. This imaginary circle passes through the North and South Poles.

Magnetic north: The direction the compass needle points.

Map aid lines: Parallel lines inside the housing of orienteering compasses. When these are aligned to map north, the compass will give a proper bearing you can follow on the ground.

Meridians: Same as lines of longitude. Meridians run true north and south.

NCIC (National Cartographic Information Service): The federal clearinghouse for special purpose maps and cartographic information.

North: There are three norths—true (geographic), magnetic (direction the compass needle points), and grid (direction the grid lines run).

Orienteering: Competitive sport combining cross-country running and compass directions to locate specific points (called controls) on the ground.

Parallels: Lines of latitude. These run "parallel" to the equator.

Planimetric map: A map that does not indicate elevation above sea level. Example, a common road map.

Protractor: A plastic arc used for measuring angles.

Scale: The relationship between map and ground distance. Expressed as a representative fraction, such as 1:250,000.

Symbols: Icons on maps that depict primarily man-made features.

Topographic map: A map that shows topography in three dimensions with the aid of contour lines.

USGS (United States Geological Survey): Place where you order topographic maps.

Variation: A nautical term for declination.

Common GPS Terms

Almanac Data: Satellite constellation information (including data about location and health) transmitted by each satellite. Your GPS receiver must acquire this information before it can begin to calculate a position.

Bearing: The compass direction from your position to your destination.

Constellation: An arrangement of objects—such as stars or satellites—in the sky.

Differential GPS (DGPS): A ground-based extension of the GPS system that uses radio beacons to transmit position corrections to GPS receivers to increase their accuracy.

Estimated Time of Arrival (ETA): The time of day when you will arrive at your destination, based on your speed of travel and remaining distance.

Estimated Time en Route (ETE): The time left before you will reach your destination if you maintain your present speed.

Grid: A coordinate system that projects the earth on a flat surface using square zones, or sets of parallel lines, for position measurements. Universal Transverse Mercator (UTM) is one example of a grid system.

Ground Speed: The speed at which you are traveling relevant to a given ground position.

Initialization: The power-up process a receiver conducts to determine its location when it hasn't been used for a long time, has been moved hundreds of miles since its last use, or has lost its correct Coordinated Universal Time.

Latitude: The north/south measurement (given in degrees) of a position perpendicular to the earth's polar axis.

Location: Where you are in the physical world. This differs from the position fix provided by your GPS receiver.

Longitude: An east/west measurement of position (given in degrees) relative to the Prime Meridian located in Greenwich, England. This

174

imaginary circle passes through the North and South Poles.

Multipath: Interference caused by the GPS satellite's radio signal bouncing off an object (such as a building, a cliff, or even wet leaves) before being received by your GPS unit.

Navigation: The process of finding your way from one place to another and knowing where you are in relation to your desired course.

Position Fix: A unique location based on a geographic coordinate system. Remember, your position fix is close to—but not the same as—your actual location in the physical world because of technology limitations and human error.

Selective Availability (SA): An error deliberately introduced into the GPS signals by the U.S. Department of Defense. Intended to deny military adversaries access to precise position information, SA skewed GPS accuracy by as much as 100 meters. SA was turned off in May 2000.

Track: The direction of travel relative to a given ground position.

Universal Transverse Mercator (UTM): A grid coordinate system that projects global sections onto a flat surface to measure position in a specific zone.

Waypoint: A specific location saved in a GPS receiver's memory.

Index

A

Aerial photos, 6–7, 14
  source for, 8–9
A-frame shelter, 139, **139**
Agonic line, defined, **46,**
  46–47, 171
Aiming off
  defined, 32, 171
  example of, 44–46, **45**
Airplane, as shelter, 144
Alders, for fires, 120
Almanac data, defined,
  74–75, 174
American maps. *See also* Maps
  common symbols of, 159
  Land Use/Land Cover, 8
  scale of, 4, 7
  sources for, 8–10
Animals, for food, **132,**
  132–36, **134**
Aspen, for fires, 120
Attack point, defined, 39, 171

B

Back bearing, defined, 171
Barrel cactus, for water, 124
Bar scale, for horizontal distances,
  24, **24**
Baseline, defined, **6,** 59, 171
Base plate, defined, 171
Bearing
  defined, 39, 171, 174
  and graduations, 34–35

magnetic bearing, 48–49, 50
map, determining with com-
  pass, 39, **40,** 41, **42,**
  43, **43**
at night, 56
taking, with fixed-dial compass,
  37, **37**
taking, with orienteering com-
  pass, 35–36, **36**
Beaver
  dam, as shelter, 141, 143
  for food, 134–35
Bezard compass, 27
Big Dipper, 58, **60**
Birch trees, for tinder, 119
Birds, for food, 132, 135
Blazer 12 (Magellan), 95
BLM. *See* Bureau of Land
  Management (BLM)
Boots, outdoor, 163
Bow-and-drill method, for fires,
  115, 115–17, **116**
Box trap, 133–34, **134**
Brunton/Lakota, Inc., orienteering
  compass, 3
Bureau of Land Management
  (BLM), 86

C

Cactus, for food, 136
Camera lens, for fires, 117, **118**
Camp, making, 137–44
  A-frame shelter, 139, **139**

evergreen bough shelter, 138, **138**

habitat as shelter, 141, 143

lean-to shelter, **137,** 137–38

tree shelter, 139, **140**

trench shelter, 140, **141, 142**

vehicles as shelter, 143–44

Canada Map Office, 9

Canadian maps. *See also* Maps

Land Use Information Series, 7–8

scale of, 4, 7

sources for, 9–10

Candles, 114

Canyons, and contour lines, 18–19, **19**

Car, as shelter, 143–44

Cardinal points (directions), 38, 171

Casio GPS WristWatch, 107

Cattails, for food, 136

Cave, as shelter, 143

Cellular phone, value of, 145

Center of Topographic Information, 9

Chinese, and first compass, 27

Cigarette lighter, use of, 115

Climate, maps showing, 7–8

Clothing

outdoor, 163

as signaling device, **147,** 148–49

Colored maps, 7

Compass, 27–37

accuracy of, 31–32

aiming off, 32, 44–46, **45,** 171

common terms of, 171–73

cost of, 35

cruiser, 29

and declination, 34, 46–50, **47, 49**

determining map bearing with, 39, **40,** 41, **42,** 43, **43**

electronic digital, 31, **31**

fixed-dial, 28, **28, 34,** 37, **37**

floating-dial, 29, **29**

graduations in, 34–35

history of, 27–28

importance of, 62

and inclination, 34

modern, 28

needle, damping, 32–33

night sights, 55

orienteering, 3, **30,** 30–31, 35–36, **36,** 41, **43**

rose, **38,** 38–39

sights, 33

styles of, compared, **34**

and triangulation, 51–53, **52**

use with GPS, 77

using stars as, 58, **60**

watch as, 58, **59**

Compass goldenrod *(Solidage nemoralis),* for direction, 63

Compass housing, defined, 172

Compass needle, damping, 32–33

Compass rose, 38–39, **39,** 171

Compass styles, compared, **34**

Constellation, 174

Contour interval. *See also* Contour lines

defined, 17–18, 171

Contour lines

defined, 16, 17–18, 84, **85,** 171

NOAA/NOS. *See* National
Oceanic and Atmospheric
Administration/National
Ocean Survey
(NOAA/NOS)
North, 173
finding with stars, 58, **60**
locating true, 14–16, **15**
North American Datum,
1927/1983, 84
North Star
determining declination by,
59, **60**
locating, 58, **60**

O

180-degree error, compass navigation, 38–39, **40**
Operation Desert Storm, and
GPS, 70
Optical sights, compass, 33, **34**
and bearing, 35
Optimus, Inc., orienteering compass, 3
Orienteering, 173
Orienteering compass, **30,**
30–31, **34**
determining bearing with,
41, **43**
and graduations, 35
sources for, 3
and triangulation, 51–53, **52**
waist-high method of sighting,
35–36, **36**

P

Pack, supplies for
seven days, 165–66

three days, 163–65
Parallels, 173. *See also* Latitude
Photos, aerial. *See* Aerial photos
Planimetric map, 6, **6,** 173
Plants
for direction, 63
edible, 136
Polaris. *See* North Star
Position dilution of precision
(PDOP), GPS, 78
Position fix, defined, 72–73, 175
Prairie dock *(Silphium terebinthi-
naceum),* for direction, 63
Prickly lettuce *(Lactuca scariola),*
for direction, 63
Prickly pear cactus, for water, 122
Protractor, 4, 173
and orienteering compass,
30–31
and triangulation, 51–53, **52**
using to determine bearing,
41, **42**

Q

Quad maps. *See* Topographic
maps
Quadrangles. *See* Topographic
maps

R

Rabbits, snaring, **132,** 133
Raft, making, 157–58, **158**
Rainwater, collecting, 124
Receiver, GPS. *See* Global
Positioning System (GPS)
Reciprocal bearing, defined, 171
River
and contour lines, 18–19, **19**

Y

About the Authors

Cliff Jacobson (*Map and Compass*) is one of North America's most respected outdoors writers and wilderness guides. A professional canoe outfitter and guide for the Science Museum of Minnesota, and a teacher of environmental science, Jacobson is the author of sixteen books and numerous educational publications.

Scottie Barnes (*Global Positioning Systems*) is the editor of GeoInfo Systems and the former editor of GPS World. She has been covering the GPS market for years from her home in Eugene, Oregon.

James Churchill (*Survival*) has written five books on trapping and hunting and has worked as a game warden. He lives in Florence, Wisconsin.